John Bryant and Michael Levin

Banking

ON OUR

Future

A PROGRAM FOR TEACHING

YOU AND YOUR KIDS ABOUT MONEY

BEACON PRESS

Boston

BEACON PRESS
25 Beacon Street
Boston, Massachusetts 02108-2892
www.beacon.org

Beacon Press books are published under the auspices of
the Unitarian Universalist Association of Congregations.

Printed in the United States of America

06 05 04 03 02   8 7 6 5 4 3 2 1

This book is printed on acid-free paper that meets
the uncoated paper ANSI/NISO specifications for
permanence as revised in 1992.

Text design and composition by Jeff Clark
at Wilsted & Taylor Publishing Services

Library of Congress Cataloging-in-Publication Data
Bryant, John.
Banking on our future : a program for teaching you and
your kids about money / John Bryant, Michael Levin.
p.   cm.
ISBN 0-8070-4717-1 (pbk. : alk. paper)
1. Parents—Finance, Personal.   2. Finance, Personal.
I. Levin, Michael (Michael S.)   II. Title.
HG179 .B793 2002
332.024-dc21
2001007697

To my mom, **JUANITA SMITH**, and my dad, **JOHNIE WILL SMITH**, who raised me; my sister, **MARA HOSKIN**, and my brother, **DAVE HARRIS**, who protected me; my goddaughter, **KIRSTIN FOUCHE**, whose future I guard; the **OPERATION HOPE** family of partners and employees; **MURRAY ZOOTA**, chairman and CEO, Fremont Investment and Loan, and cofounder of Banking on Our Future; and every child in America who dares to dream of a future fulfilled

And to **CHYNNA BRACHA LEVIN**, and her generation

CONTENTS

PART 4

THE FINANCIALLY LITERATE

HIGH SCHOOL STUDENT

PART 5

FINANCIAL FITNESS FOR YOUNG ADULTS

PART 1

Making Sense Out of Dollars: A Guide for Adults

CHAPTER 1

Giving You the Power

Banking on Our Future banker volunteer: "Does anyone know what 'ATM' means?"

Fourth-grade student: "All the money!"

I want to empower you to talk with your children about money. This book is about taking your life back, and creating the kind of life you want—for you, your children, and your family.

Most of us don't know how to have conversations about financial issues with our kids. The purpose of this book is to show you how, whether your kids attend elementary school, middle school, or high school. We're going to see that in our society, black and white aren't nearly as important as another color—green. Together, we're going to educate your kids about money: how to get it, keep it, protect it, make it grow, and put it to work. This is more than an adventure for you and your family. In today's world, it is an absolute *necessity*.

Corporate America constantly bombards everyone in our society with messages that emphasize consuming, spending, and living. The groups least able to counter the effects of those financially destabilizing messages are inner-city young people. These youths have the least amount of access to information about financial literacy. They don't know—and all too often, neither do their parents. For children and parents alike, "It's what they don't know that they don't know that's killing them."

Learning how to handle money ought to be as vital a part of education as reading and writing for all of our young people. Children growing up in the inner city—and those of middle-class families eking by on $25,000 or $30,000 a year or less—are at risk of losing any hope of a solid financial future from bad habits learned early. Our culture's cynical barrage of images has brainwashed them into believing that the right car, clothes, and shoes are all you need to succeed.

Making it in America requires a lot more than trendy appearances. It requires information. Upper-middle-class kids constantly receive messages, both overt and subliminal, about the value of a dollar: Of course you're going to college. Of course you'll have a career. Of course you'll own your own home. Of course you'll provide for your children's education, and of course you'll save for your retirement.

Inner-city and first-generation, middle-class families simply don't have the history of money knowledge to pass on to their kids. As a result, their kids are virtually powerless against the images they see in advertisements and entertainment, from television commercials to music videos. They have little knowledge to combat the intense peer pressure that makes them feel miserable if they don't have what's cool "right now." On some level, everyone in society feels a need to "keep up with the Joneses." The middle class at least has the information to make choices about whether to succumb to the temptation to spend, spend, spend. And yet approximately half of all American families are living paycheck to paycheck. That's scary, because these poor financial planners are the same parents and families producing children who are prime candidates for corporate America. The people who need this book have no barrier between themselves and a society that benefits from keeping them on the "live-for-today" treadmill.

In our society, many businesses benefit from the lack of basic financial literacy among the poor and struggling middle class. Overly aggressive credit card companies charge exorbitant interest rates. Sneaker manufacturers advertise their product as a necessity. Collection agencies wage an incessant battle with our self-esteem. The list goes on and on. All of these industries would suffer crippling blows if inner-city America suddenly got smart about money. Ironically, America's economy would skyrocket if the unempowered gained knowledge about how money and banking really work. Renters would become homeowners, free to invest the equity in their homes as they saw fit. The rate of personal bankruptcy would dramatically decline. New markets for useful consumer goods from furniture to appliances would develop. America would be a better and richer—not to mention fairer—place if *everyone* could participate knowledgeably in the worlds of business and personal finance.

The information in this book—from righting your current financial status to preparing for the future—will revolutionize parents' ability to educate their kids and give them a leg up on the future. Without this information, our kids are doomed to reenact patterns of poverty. With this knowledge, these same children can live their dreams.

GETTING RIGHT WITH MONEY

I believe that the Bible will help you get right with God. This book will offer specific guidance for parents with children of different age groups, providing lessons and illustrating examples of how to get right with money. Everything in our culture emphasizes getting and spending, deriving self-esteem through the right consumer goods, and valuing the material over the spiritual. As Carrie Fisher wrote in *Postcards from the Edge*, "The problem with instant gratification is that it isn't fast enough."

That's what our kids believe today, and parents, especially those of you who struggle economically, face a daunting task when you try to teach your kids how to handle money. Financial literacy is an absolutely vital skill for children, especially children of color, because if they can't take care of their money when they're young, they'll never be able to take care of themselves as adults.

Businesses and credit card issuers target young people today as never before. Peer pressure to get and spend is at an all-time high.

Banking on Our Future

Kids are spending their teenage years working long hours to contribute to their families' finances and to pay for consumer goods that have little long-term meaning. No other generation of young people has been in need of financial literacy skills as the current one.

The problem is that you as a parent may not know how to address these issues because you yourself may not have grown up with financially literate role models. Your family may not have a tradition of saving and investing. It may actually be easier for you to talk with your kid about sex than to talk about money!

This book will equip you with the key information you need to teach your children to manage their money wisely. It is full of how-to illustrations and hands-on facts so that you can educate your kids (and yourself!).

Kids need to discover that saving their money means they can accomplish more in life. Children from low-income backgrounds especially often don't realize that they possess the power to own their own home, start their own business, or become leaders in their community. All too often they are unaware of how to avoid the traps of credit card debt and compulsive spending that ensnare so many millions of Americans. In this book, I want to show parents and children exactly what they need to know and do in order to attain financial self-sufficiency.

FAMILY FINANCIAL SUMMITS

The book is shaped as a series of conversation topics between parents and children. Each chapter introduces a new issue—such as "Star Charts" for your first grader and credit cards for your teenager—that you are encouraged to use as the basis for what I like to call family financial summits. These are meetings you can have each week with your kids to educate them about different aspects of financial literacy, depending on their age, stage, and interest level. The book begins with chapters aimed at increasing your own awareness about financial literacy so that you can fill in whatever gaps currently exist in your knowledge base.

The goals of this book are to show you as a parent how to:

- motivate and give license to your children to "dare to dream";
- help your children understand the importance of checking and savings accounts, budgeting, personal credit, investments, and other economic tools;
- teach your children that they can take responsibility for their lives; and
- aid your children in achieving economic literacy so that they can function knowledgeably in the financial marketplace.

How important is it for young people to achieve financial literacy? In a study conducted in the year 2000 by the JumpStart Coalition and the National Endowment for Financial Education, students from all levels of the socioeconomic spectrum were asked thirty multiple-choice questions on money management, saving, investment, and credit. The results: the average score was 51.9 percent—a failing grade. Only 6.7 percent of the students achieved a grade of "C" or higher.

Financial education is not taught in schools today, and the results of this lack are all around us: a consumer culture; staggering levels of personal unsecured debt; a sad reliance on government assistance on the part of the poor and elderly; a minuscule savings rate; and a shockingly high rate of personal bankruptcy—over a million individual bankruptcies a year. The bottom line: not just poor people need financial intervention, but it's safe to say that the poor need it more than anyone else.

WHAT QUALIFIES ME TO WRITE THIS BOOK?

I'll get more into my own story as we go on, but a few basics are in order here. I grew up in Compton, California, and South Central Los Angeles. My parents divorced when I was young, but I grew up with a father who owned his own business (he still owns it after fifty years), and I watched him meet his payroll every week. My mother has worked hard all of her life, and although we were often broke, we were never poor. To this day, I remain grateful for the love my parents have shown me—and for their being wise financial role models.

I started my first business when I was ten years old, selling candy in my neighborhood after school. I went down to the corner liquor store and told the owner two things: First, he was selling the wrong kind of candy! Second, my friends had to go out of their way to buy candy from his store, which made them late for school, and they were getting pink slips as a result. I offered to help him solve these problems and make more money. He said, "Go away, little boy. I have a college degree."

I said to him, "But I'm ten years old, and I buy candy. I know what I'm talking about. I have cavities to prove it. You're selling the wrong kind of candy. The only reason that people buy your candy is that there's no other place to go. There's no competition."

He said, "Go away, little boy."

I said, "Can you hire me as a box boy? I need a job."

He said, "Okay."

I said, "Can you show me how you buy wholesale and sell retail? I'm just curious."

Six months later, I bummed forty bucks off my mother and I opened the neighborhood candy house in my den, made $300 a week, and put the liquor store out of the candy business. My candy house was on the way to school. People ask me, how could you, at ten years of age, have the chutzpah to start your own business? And my only response is, it never dawned on me that I couldn't. Because my father had done it before me, I had the immigrant work ethic. I had my father's sense of *Yes, I can*. I had my mother behind me with her supreme self-confidence and love. These lessons have stood me in good stead, even at my lowest.

By accident rather than design, I became a teenage actor. Before long, I was living the high life in Malibu, California, sharing a beachfront home with friends. I wasn't quite eighteen, and I was making it as a performer. But my attitude grew faster than my acting abilities, and soon I found myself unemployed and living in the back of my Jeep behind an old Italian restaurant near LAX.

While I was waiting tables in Malibu, I had the good fortune to meet a businessman who became my mentor and launched me in the worlds of banking and business. Within a few short years, I went from the back of that Jeep to engineering a management buyout of a company.

By the age of twenty-six, I had met the president of the United States, I was completing multimillion-dollar banking deals, and I was enjoying life as a successful California entrepreneur. I'd love to say that months in advance I predicted the Rodney King verdict, and the ensuing aftermath of violence and destruction. I should have seen it coming. But I didn't. In fact, I'd gotten so caught up in my own wealth and success that the verdict—and the civil unrest that followed—completely astonished me.

Shame on me.

My life was going so well, I didn't believe there would be a riot. Of course, like everyone else in the country, I'd seen the videotape of Rodney King getting beaten by those cops. But I'd shrugged it off because I believed in my heart that justice would prevail, and those cops would be punished for their horrible actions.

We live in America, I told myself as I headed to work on the day the verdict came down. We have a Constitution and a Bill of Rights. And hey, I'm doing well, so what's your problem? I figured that the jury would convict the cops, and life would go on. It never occurred to me that anything different might happen.

And then the verdicts came down. I remember it was four o'clock in the afternoon on April 29. I was looking out at the city from my eighth-floor office suite, and the city was on fire. I felt hollow, like a fraud.

I had expected that the government was somehow going to take care of business. And it didn't. The verdict allowing those officers to go free was a horrible miscarriage of justice.

Banking on Our Future

I looked at myself and decided that if I wasn't part of the solution, I was damn well part of the problem. I couldn't blame the government, the mayor, or any of the myriad other people involved. *What the hell have you done, John? You lived in Compton and South Central Los Angeles. Now you live in a house in the hills. You grew up, grew out, and left. And now look at yourself, John. You blame poverty on the poor.*

And then it dawned on me. The way to prevent such turmoil in the future would be to turn the residents of South Central, Compton, and Watts—the areas of L.A. most devastated by the civil unrest—into stakeholders in their community. Make them *homeowners* instead of renters.

I knew the cost of housing in the inner city. I knew that if you could scrape together the down payment, the monthly mortgage payment would be no more than what you were paying in rent. I understood that three problems stood in the way: First, inner-city residents had little access to or knowledge of the banking system. Second, many had problematic credit histories or no credit histories at all. They would have been turned down in a flash by any conventional bank. And third, most major banks had zero interest in developing a customer base in the inner city.

At that moment, Operation HOPE was born. The dream: To turn inner-city residents into homeowners and stakeholders. To bring them knowledge of the banking system and to show them how to be savvy banking consumers. To teach young people in the inner city the same lessons about money, personal finance, and banking that the children of wealthy families take for granted. To give the poor not simply civil rights, but *silver rights*, too.

To date, Operation HOPE has facilitated more than $94 million in commitments for inner-city loans, homeownership, and small-business ownership to poor folks who would not otherwise have qualified for a loan. Established in April 1996, our Banking on Our Future Program, with national chapters in cities across the United States, has educated 87,000 kids in the basics of checking and savings accounts and the importance of credit and investments.

Giving You the Power

And we've had great success in changing young people's lives. One of my favorite stories is of Ariana, a young Latina, all of twelve years old. She took the Banking on Our Future classes and then went home and started asking her parents questions. Well, because young Ariana was of her family's first English-speaking generation, she paid the household bills. Up until this point, she had simply done what her parents told her: taking cash from the cookie jar, or from underneath the mattress, and going to the local check cashier to purchase money orders, which Ariana then paid bills with. But not after Ariana gained an economic education through Banking on Our Future with the great team of banker-teachers that go into inner-city classrooms. She started asking questions and, better yet, doing the math.

Ariana discovered not only that the family was paying a steep price for operating outside of the traditional mainstream financial system—the annual cost of "fringe" banking services averages $199 to $444 compared to $100 for a traditional checking account (Robert Manning, Poverty & Race Research Action Council, 1999) —but also that, because of her age and lack of knowledge about money, she was probably being taken advantage of by the local check-cashing operation where the family sent her to do business. Well, in short order Ariana started teaching her parents and siblings about the power of money and about the mainstream banking system. She explained to her family how banks in the United States were different from banks in Mexico, where they had had a number of bad experiences. She gained her family's confidence and, with the help of her teacher at school, proceeded to open both a savings account and a checking account, which (again with her teacher's help) she then used to pay family bills.

At twelve years of age, Ariana gained the respect of her elders, took control of her family's financial future, and helped to set the entire family firmly on the right track for their collective and individual futures. This is what economic literacy can do.

My experience, as founder of Operation HOPE and Banking on Our Future, and as an entrepreneur, banker, and son of Compton, will inform this book. I hope that by sharing my knowledge, I will give you a crash course in the fundamentals of economic literacy that will enable you to teach your children how to make money a servant and not a master. Let's change our children's future—and ours—for the better.

CHAPTER 2

How to Be a Good Financial Role Model for Your Kids

Along with reading, mathematics, and computer literacy, financial literacy is a critical component in the ultimate success of our students in the twenty-first century.

KATHERINE NELSON, BANKING ON OUR FUTURE

INSTRUCTIONAL COORDINATOR

There's an old Southern saying: "No matter how much I love you, my child, if I don't have wisdom, all I can give you is my own ignorance." Out of love, we often pass down bad habits from one generation to the next. Your job, as CEO of your household and financial guru for your children, is to draw the line as to what is acceptable and what is not.

Before we can start teaching our kids about money, we have to examine our own attitude toward it. Both wealthy and poor families have one surprising trait in common: parents do not spend much time discussing money with their kids. The difference comes in the expectations. In financially wealthy families, children grow up believing that they are entitled to be rich. There is an expectation that they will complete their education, land a financially secure job, earn a lot of money, buy a big house, drive nice cars, and so on. They view money as a tool toward having a wonderful, fulfilling life.

For poor, working-, and lower-middle-class families, there are no such expectations. Parents in poor or working-class families often foster negative notions about money in their children. These parents may harbor resentment toward others who are better-off or had greater opportunities for education or work. They view money as negative, almost dirty. Rich people have gotten that way only by cheating or being dishonest. Even some wealthy people believe that "behind every great fortune is a crime."

That message can be reinforced in surprising and unconscious ways, even in church. Many believe, incorrectly, that the Bible states, "Money is the root of all evil." That's not what it says, my friend. The Bible actually says, "*Love of* money is the root of all evil." In other words, when we love money for its own sake above all else, that's when we run into trouble.

Here's a little quiz. Fill in the blank: Money is _____.

What's the first thing that came to your mind? Was it positive or negative? What are your attitudes about money? What attitudes are you consciously or unconsciously passing on to your kids? The first lesson to learn about money is that it is neutral. It is simply a form of exchange, a system with which to barter our labor and ideas for the goods and services of others. Having or lacking money doesn't make you a better or worse person.

Sometimes, in justifying our own lack of money, we tell ourselves that those who are well-off are somehow morally flawed, having obtained their wealth through the time-honored ethics of lie-cheat-steal. It's hard to maintain such an attitude without sharing it with our children.

Teaching our kids to be of good character is the most important thing we can do, but we need to emphasize that being of good character includes being responsible about money! Society often makes it sound as if you must choose between being spiritual and being financially successful. I'm here to tell you that's false. You can have your cake and eat it, too. One does not have to exclude the other.

How to Be a Good Financial Role Model for Your Kids

The key is to remember that money is a tool, and not the key to happiness.

Certainly many of the wealthy role models in the public eye are not positive examples, especially for kids. Every music video I have seen depicts success as a fancy car, attractive women, champagne, and all the other trappings of wealth. I have yet to see a rap video of a twenty-two-year-old singer studying *The Wall Street Journal* to figure out what the next investment should be for his retirement plan! It may not be sexy, but it's real.

DELAYED GRATIFICATION

Just because we're not Donald Trump doesn't mean that we're not a success. The most important lesson you can teach your children is how to be a positive role model. You need to instill in them the concept of delayed gratification — it's okay to work hard for a goal that seems far off. Today, from the streets of Harlem to the gated enclaves of Bel Air, most high school students have jobs. However, unlike past generations, today's high school students generally are not working to help support their families. Instead, they are working to buy themselves the clothing and music that their friends have.

In addition to beginning their resume at an early age, working students learn the value of a dollar through their own experience. The problem comes when kids are working solely to buy the material items they deem essential to their peers. By doing so, they are taking precious, irreplaceable hours away from activities that seem much more boring and mundane — homework, extracurricular activities, volunteering — and that are absolutely essential. Such pastimes can make the difference between getting accepted to college and being left behind.

Let's take a look at the average week of a high school student. School days average seven hours, or thirty-five hours a week. Twenty hours a week at a part-time job brings that number up to fifty-five hours. Add in an hour each day for commuting to school and work, and we hit the sixty-hour mark. Very few *adults* work sixty-hour weeks. When a teenager works those kinds of hours, how much time is left over for schoolwork, socializing, or sleep? Not enough!

A part-time job can instill a good work ethic and notions of responsibility and time management at an early age. However, unless that income is unquestionably needed, you are having your child put short-term gain ahead of long-term success. Teenagers are painfully dependent on the opinions of others for their own self-esteem. It's awfully hard to convince a teenager that volunteering at County Hospital is as "cool" as making eight dollars an hour selling retail at the mall.

Money is not so important that our kids should be sacrificing their education—and their childhood. They will be adults for the rest of their lives, with plenty of opportunity to earn a living later on.

UNEQUAL COMPARISONS

We need to understand that we are not putting our children at a disadvantage simply because we are unable to provide every single toy, experience, or trip that wealthier parents can. A firm moral foundation and the knowledge of how to take care of themselves financially are far more valuable gifts than a trust fund and a Ferrari on your child's eighteenth birthday.

For most parents, it's a terrible struggle to see your kids operating on financial values that are so different from your own—and so clearly unhealthy for them. It's painful to see our kids caught up in a spiral of getting and spending. It almost feels as though their lives are not their own. Parents are often bewildered when a child feels it's so important to have a particular kind of outfit or gear.

The answer involves a bit of psychology. When children reach the early teen years, they are at a stage of development when they no longer take cues from their parents. Instead, they start taking cues from their peers, the boys and girls their own age. This represents their first step in moving out from the emotional dominance of their parents and beginning to establish themselves as adults in their own right.

Parents must recognize that this phase is not only necessary, it's *healthy*. Unfortunately, this knowledge doesn't make it any easier to live with a teenager who is constantly criticizing his or her parents. It's no walk in the park.

This problem is further exacerbated by the way parents are portrayed in popular culture. In most families, the TV is on from early in the morning until late at night, acting as a combination of electronic babysitter and source of stimulation. The problem with TV is that in many of the shows, especially those geared for kids or lower-income families, parents are portrayed as absolute fools. On everything from *The Simpsons* to *Moesha*, children treat their parents rudely. As a parent, you are competing for the attention of your child with a TV culture that makes you look foolish, square, and so far behind the times that you don't even know what time it is. Even though there are plenty of educational offerings on TV, by and large, kids don't want to watch them. They want to watch the sitcoms where nobody is more foolish than Mom and Dad.

If you're not ready to part with your beloved television, then you can take steps to monitor the shows that your children watch. Lay down the law about how much television is allowed, what shows are forbidden, and what shows you will watch with them.

By instilling basic values and financial knowledge in your children at a young age, you provide them with the requisite information to successfully manage their financial assets the rest of their lives. Proper preparation for the world outside the shelter of your roof offers a much more level playing field in the real world.

In order to help our children, we need to examine our own relationship to money. We have to investigate whether we believe it's a good thing or a bad thing. We need to eradicate the belief that being spiritual and being financially comfortable are mutually exclusive. We have to see that corporate America is absolutely thrilled to have our kids join the working and consuming classes at the earliest possible age.

Banking on Our Future

HOW TIMES HAVE CHANGED

Forty years ago, the greatest threat to American blacks came from a society that denied us the basic civil rights that we and our children today take for granted. In my lifetime, blacks could be turned away from lunch counters or any other place of business simply because of the color of our skin. Thank God for leaders such as Martin Luther King, Jr., Andrew Young, the NAACP, and so many others who risked and often surrendered their lives for equality.

Sometimes those who sought to take the civil rights—or the lives—of blacks wore the bedsheets of the Ku Klux Klan. Sometimes they wore police uniforms, wielded batons and guns, and went accompanied by attack dogs. Either way, we always knew who the enemy was.

Today, the biggest enemy of self-sufficiency and financial well-being for blacks, and indeed for the working poor and lower middle class, is much more indistinct. Today, the enemy is anyone who passes on to his or her children a combination of good intentions and lack of knowledge about how to be self-sufficient. In other words, increasingly we are our own problem.

We are the problem if we do not know how to teach our children the value of a dollar. We are the problem if we do not teach our children that it is not how much money you make that matters, but how much you keep. We are the problem if we fail to teach our kids that economic literacy is every bit as important as geometry. We are the problem if we don't demand more from our banks when they fail to meet our needs. I have nothing against right triangles or the elements of the periodic table, but there's a whole lot more to life that neither the schools nor parents are teaching kids.

In the twenty-first century, we cannot afford to be lukewarm with our intentions. That's as bad as the people—fellow ecumenical leaders, at that—who bitterly criticized Dr. King when he was jailed for fighting racism in Birmingham, Alabama. Good intentions, which I define as being lukewarm, are driving low- to moderate-income citizens everywhere, into the poorhouse. The road to hell —and bankruptcy—is paved with good intentions.

The bottom line here is this: you can only give what you've got. This chapter asks the question "What have you got?" Mentally. Spiritually. Emotionally. Economically. What do you have to pass down to your children about financial literacy, and about life?

Ask yourself these four questions: How much do you earn? How much do you save? How much do you spend? How much do you owe?

The main obstacle holding you back isn't Birmingham's Bull Conner and his baton-wielding goons. The biggest problem that we face on the road to becoming financially strong is vagueness. Most of us simply don't know how much we earn, save, spend, and owe. We have a vague sense of these numbers, but we are not entirely sure, often because we don't want to know. The true numbers can be depressing!

Don't feel bad if you couldn't answer the four questions off the top of your head. You are in very good company. But how can this be?

BLAME IT ON THE GAP

In my hometown of Los Angeles, one men's clothing store constantly runs an ad that has the owner of the store saying, at the end, "You are going to love the way you look. I guarantee it." His testimonial implies that buying his clothes will make you feel good about yourself. Now, I like this particular clothier, and I even shop there, but on closer inspection, you might begin to sense that he's implying you couldn't possibly love the way you look right now. If you did, you wouldn't need his clothes. All advertising aims to make the same point: not only is their stuff good, but your stuff is worthless. Of course, most of us don't go out and buy a new car every six months, and we don't throw out all our clothing and buy a whole new wardrobe every time we see a Gap ad on TV. But it's hard to look at so much stuff on television and not wish that we could some-how afford it all so that we could look as happy as the paid actors in the commercials. If it's hard for us to overcome such corporate-induced urges, imagine how much harder it is for our kids, who live by the opinions of their peers.

Almost every parent has endured the trying task of back-to-school shopping, during which we discover that our children have ex-tremely fixed—and expensive—ideas about what their classmates will deem acceptable. They wouldn't be caught dead in the old, old hand-me-downs their older siblings wore not two years ago. (No matter that your own wardrobe looks virtually the same as when you moved out of your parents' house.) From your kids' point of view, fashion becomes a life-or-death issue. Kids are merciless with each other. Wearing the wrong jeans to school can label you an outcast before the first bell rings. I am talking from personal experience, my friend! My mother used to dress me in handmade suits that served only to get me beat up on the way home from school every day. Home-stitched copies of Little Lord Fauntleroy suits, to be exact. One of my least favorite was a three-piece, burgundy, crush-velvet job, complete with ruffled shirt and a big, big, big bow tie! My dear mother, I later found out, was "crazy like a fox." She and my father probably saved my life, if not my butt. Maybe they dressed me funny, but they sure instilled the right values in me. Which ac-counts for why I now appreciate what they did, but not then. Groups don't succeed, individuals do, and my parents were intent on grow-ing an individual.

At eight, I didn't want to wear those outfits. I wanted to wear the cool threads I saw on TV, in the stores, and on the kids who knew how to put some money together, one way or another. Yes, kids know what they "have to have," and it doesn't come cheap.

SETTING AN EXAMPLE

Most of us, rich or poor, adults or kids, look at our personal finances from the point of view not of "What can I afford to buy myself?" but of "I've got to have this *now*, no matter what it does to my savings!" Often, when we feel blue, we buy items we might not be able to afford, either so that we can look rich or so that we simply feel better about ourselves for the moment. These habits are mighty tough to break. So the question is this: How can we become strong financial role models for our children? We will always be swimming against the tide of adolescent and teen peer pressure, but we have to make a stand nonetheless. Let's take a look at some painless ways to examine our own financial situation so that we can make sure we are passing on the right messages to our kids.

You might want to take out a blank piece of paper and follow along as we do a brief financial checkup together.

1. **What is your annual take-home income?** I am not talking about your published annual pay or salary. I am talking about what you actually deposit into your bank or hide under the bed, the total amount you write checks against or deduct via the ATM (automatic teller machine). This is our starting point. Perhaps you have a second job or income in the form of alimony or child support. Total it all up right here, so that you have a precise number that represents exactly what you bring in each year. Now, this is between you and you—you don't have to tell anyone what this number is. But if you are going to be serious, you need to start off knowing exactly how much money you have to play with in any given year.

2. **How much do you save?** Another way to phrase this question is to ask, "How much do you pay yourself?" Most of us are so consumed with catching up with bills and keeping the lights on that we neglect to save for the future. It can seem downright impossible to do when there are so many financial demands here and now.

There was a time in my life when I was living in the back of my Jeep, so I am not one to scold about your financial habits. I struggled and was fortunate enough to find some success. No matter what your current financial situation, make a new commitment: *Pay yourself first.* From now on, 10 percent of every dollar that you take in should go directly to savings. Pay yourself before you pay the gas company, Visa, or the magazine subscription. Take that money directly out of your paycheck and stick it in a savings plan, either with the bank or, if your employer offers it, in a 401(k) program. Stick it under the mattress, for all I care. But get that 10 percent out of your hands and into your savings.

This is not purely a financial commitment—it's a spiritual and emotional commitment as well. When you start putting 10 percent of your money into savings, several important changes occur on a psychological level. First, you are telling yourself that there really is more than enough. You are demonstrating to yourself that you are so well taken care of that you can actually afford to set some money aside for later. This is an extremely important message to give yourself. The alternative, where we take every dime and immediately kick it out to our various creditors and collection agencies, reinforces the belief that we work for everyone *but* ourselves. We work for the phone company. We work for the gas company. We work for the grocery store. But we don't really work for ourselves. Putting 10 percent of your money directly into savings changes everything. It gives you a sense that you truly matter, that you deserve to keep some of your hard-earned money. It says, "I love me enough to invest in me first!"

In the 1920s, George Clason wrote a book called *The Richest Man in Babylon*. I urge you to find a copy of that book and study it, as it has helped millions of Americans achieve their financial dreams. In that book, Clason came up with a key phrase: "A part of all I earn is mine to keep." When you start putting money aside, you feel good about yourself in a way that you cannot imagine. It's said that money in the bank gives a peace of mind that surpasses all understanding. Once you start letting those dollars add up in a savings account, you will feel a sense of building for the future—not simply getting by in the here and now.

Every time I receive a paycheck, in my mind I immediately discount its value by 10 percent. It stops being $1,000 and starts being $900. It wasn't $2,500, it was $2,250. So put that first 10 percent of your income directly into savings. This is true regardless of what your current bills add up to.

This leads us to our next question.

3. How much do you spend? The key to happiness: *Spend less than you make.* Any questions? Am I going too fast?

Spending is the area where just about everyone in America suffers from financial amnesia. We spend money but have absolutely no recollection of where it went. We remember putting a lot of cash into our wallet, only to discover a few days later that it's seemingly vanished. Where did it go? "Money talks," goes the expression. "It says good-bye." In my experience, money doesn't even say good-bye. It just up and leaves. Where exactly does it go? Your next task is to find out just that.

Buy a pad of accountant ledger paper, which is divided into columns and rows so you can keep track of financial items. (If you're unsure what accountant ledger paper looks like, ask a clerk in an office supply store; he or she will know exactly what you mean.) For the next month, use this pad to write down *every dime you spend.* Whether you are making a mortgage payment or buying a newspaper, write it down. For your record keeping, I suggest these categories:

- Food
- Home (rent or mortgage, heat, gas, water, etc.)
- Clothing
- Personal Care (medical bills, drugstore purchases, etc.)
- Cards and Gifts
- Savings
- Charitable Donations
- Transportation (car payment, gas, registration, repairs, bus, subway, etc.)
- Miscellaneous (CDs, household items, etc.)
- Debt Payments

Add a few other columns as pertain to your particular situation. After a couple of days of writing down how much you spend in each of these categories, something amazing will happen: you'll find yourself not spending money on things you'd be too embarrassed to write down! Simply by keeping track of where your money goes, you'll find yourself making wiser decisions about spending. You might have been wondering where you were going to find that 10 percent of your income to put in savings as I suggested above. Well, you'll find a lot of that 10 percent right here. It will become crystal clear to you, as it has to me, exactly how much money you spend unnecessarily. As the prophet Isaiah asked, "Why do you spend money on things that are not bread?" In other words, why do we spend money on things that don't really matter to us?

The answer is that sometimes we just don't want to think about how little we may really have. Self-esteem cannot be purchased; it comes only when we have the self-respect to protect our financial future by saving instead of splurging and wasting. You'll find that by keeping careful track of all your spending, you will stop spending on unnecessary items. You won't even desire that button at the car wash that says, "I spend money I don't have, on things I don't even want, to impress people I don't even like." If that's your philosophy of life, then you'll find things change radically once you commit to writing your spending down.

Examining spending patterns to determine where money is not being used to its maximum effectiveness is a skill that will pay off dividends for decades. Think about Starbucks. People line up to spend as much as $4 for a cup of coffee every morning. That's $20 a week, $80 a month, almost $1,000 a year! Once you realize how much money you're frittering away, you can learn to curb such small indulgences.

4. How much do you owe? If you are like most people in this society, you owe—and you owe *a lot*. Few of us can resist those "free" credit cards (now, isn't that an oxymoron!) that announce our very own credit limit of $5,000. Somehow we confuse the idea of "credit limit" and "outright gift"! The problem with using credit cards is that we eventually have to pay the money back—despite the wishes of our credit card company. Every time you make a purchase with a credit card, the credit card company gets a fee of 2 to 3 percent of the purchase price. In other words, if you use your Visa to purchase $100 worth of CDs, Visa gets about $2.50 from the merchant. But that's not where they make their real money. Visa really begins to rake in the dough with the 18 to 20 percent annual interest they charge if you do not pay off your balance in full every month. Credit card issuers *hate* it when people pay off their balances! They can't make a dime that way.

Fortunately for our creditors, most of us simply make the minimum payment and continue to spend, while our debt continues to grow from a molehill into a mountain. It's possible for a family to spend as much on minimum payments for a credit card as for any other item in their monthly spending plan, including rent, mortgage, or food. Unscrupulous credit card companies are like drug dealers who hang around schoolyards: they have no mercy, and their gain comes as a result of your paying. But the truth is we have no one to blame but ourselves if we get into trouble with credit cards. Credit cards are not free money. If anything, they can be the most expensive kind of spending because we end up paying for a good or service many times over if we do not pay off our balance.

One of the absolute worst uses for your credit card is a vacation. Many people charge up their cards and tell themselves they'll work extra hard over the next few months in order to pay it off. Let me tell you from experience that there's nothing worse than paying off a vacation you've already taken. However, a close runner-up is making payments on a car that no longer runs. Ouch. Yes, I have done that one also.

Stop using credit cards as much as possible. Cut them up and throw them out to avoid the temptation to do financial damage to yourself. Then, with the possibility of accumulating more credit card debt out of the way, the next step in our quest for plastic emancipation is to reduce your credit card debt every month. The best suggestion that financial experts offer is to take a second 10 percent, after savings, and put that toward paying off credit cards. Consult your accountant ledger pad for other areas where you can find that money. You'll find that the unnecessary purchases you are cutting out of your life will be more than adequate to pay for both the 10 percent of savings and the 10 percent for credit card payments.

Some people feel they should postpone saving until they have paid off all of their credit card debt. I always reply with a resounding "No." Do both at the same time. You'll find that both practices are addictive. The more you save, the more you'll want to save. The more you pay off your credit cards, the more you'll want to pay them off. Before you know it, your financial picture will be much stronger.

BUDGET SCHMUDGET

People often ask me how they can establish a budget for themselves and their families. I find budgets to be a lot like diets: they're a lot easier to start than to stick to. I myself have a budget, and I work hard to stay within it (give or take 10 to 15 percent wiggle room every month). Once you start writing down your spending, you'll have a pretty good idea of where the money goes. You'll then be able to judge in any given month whether your spending in a particular area was higher or lower than usual. You can go back and ask yourself why, and you can reduce any unnecessary spending in that area. Most people find this system to be more successful than a budget, which is awfully hard to keep.

Blowing a budget is a lot like blowing a diet. You can diet all day long and suddenly find yourself eating a piece of chocolate cake at night. You figure that the diet is blown anyway and you'll start again tomorrow . . . so you finish off the cake. The same is true with budgets. We end up spending a certain amount of money on a frill, then scold ourselves for blowing our budget. We then rationalize that since we've already blown it, we might as well blow it *with style*. Before we know it, we've practically melted the MasterCard.

Rather than get on that fateful cycle of commitment, stick to tracking your finances. Your budget will naturally evolve from those ledger pad numbers. For those of you up to the task, and if your family can afford a computer, I'd even recommend going one step beyond the ledger pad and investing in a personal finance program, such as Quicken. (There are several financial management applications to choose from, but since I have been using Quicken for nearly ten years, I can fully endorse it.) The average family will have no problem mastering Quicken, which can be used to keep track of checking accounts and any other savings vehicles. Because the program is so widely used, many banks and financial institutions offer ways to download account information directly into Quicken, making it even more attractive.

For further credit help, call Operation HOPE (888-572-HOPE) and speak to one of our credit counselors. Our experts will analyze your situation and attempt to place you in a local credit counseling and financial planning program in your area. There's no shame in getting help with your money. The only shame is being less than 100 percent financially responsible and doing nothing about it.

You don't need an M.B.A.; you need only a firm grasp of how much you earn, save, spend, and owe. If you know those four amounts, you will have taken a giant step on the road toward economic self-sufficiency—and a giant leap toward becoming an ideal financial role model for your kids.

CHAPTER 3

Keeping It All Together

There was a time I was so broke I couldn't pay attention.

JOHN BRYANT

BILLS, BILLS, AND MORE BILLS

Most people would rather have their fingernails pulled out one by one than talk about paying bills, let alone actually *pay* them. We associate bill paying with pain, especially if we don't have all that much money to begin with. Many people allow bills to pile up until they start coming in different colors—red, green, purple, blue—all the colors of the bill collector's rainbow. When the Reverend Jesse Jackson talks about a Rainbow Coalition, he is not talking about the color of your bill.

One of my friends refers to bills as "TV mail" because your address looks like it's inside a tiny TV set (actually the windowed envelope the bill comes in). Unfortunately, bills don't come with an option of changing the channel, or even turning down the volume.

Since we can't avoid bills (at least not forever), we need to find a healthy, sensible way to deal with them. The key thing to remember is that the companies that generate bills don't want your money. They want *their* money. People who are sending you bills are people who have already provided you a service or a product, whether it's last month's electricity or the car you drive to work each day. As a courtesy, we can at least not delay in giving them what they've actually earned. You'd be mad as hell if your boss suddenly said, "You know, I'm not going to pay you just now for the work you've already done. Why don't you come back in three weeks? Better yet, make that two months. I'll pay you then . . . if I feel like it." None of us would stay with an employer who treated us like that. And yet we turn around and act the same way toward our creditors.

Common courtesy aside, failure to pay your bills can result in some unpleasant situations. Companies quickly run out of compassion for people who don't pay their bills and won't communicate. The phone company won't call and say, "We really hate to do this, but we're going to have to turn your phone off. So if you want to make a few last calls before we flip the switch, you might want to do it now." If you don't pay, they won't play. It's as simple as that.

Aside from being humiliating, getting your services reconnected is both expensive and time consuming. Not to mention the whole unpleasant process they put you through. Meanwhile, your kids are wondering why the lights are off again or why the phone doesn't work. On top of all that, there are late fees. At the end of the whole mess, we end up paying far more for services than if we had simply paid the bill when it arrived.

Get past this stage in your life. You don't need the hassle. I'd like to suggest that you collect all your bills and pay them—every other week. Pay them in full. As long as you have money in the bank, write the checks and get those bills out the door—less 10 percent, of course!

SEEING RED

Unfortunately, sometimes we just don't have enough money to pay a particular bill. When faced with such a dilemma, many of us simply act as if the situation didn't exist. We throw out the bill or ignore it altogether, as if by doing so would make the matter disappear. We need to understand that creditors do *not* want to punish you or send you to jail. All they want is their money, which they'll have no hopes of getting if you're locked behind bars. So what do you do in such a situation?

Believe it or not, you call them. Tell them exactly what your situation is. Explain that you are a regular customer and that this month things are a little tight. Ask if you can either skip the payment or make a minimum payment. Most creditors will be happy to arrange an easy set of terms for you. Our fear of creditors stems from the more common experience of their chasing us down—a situation that requires them to spend more money just to get out of us what is rightfully theirs. Of course they're angry. You would be, too, if you had to play hide-and-seek with your boss to get your paycheck.

If you take the initiative to contact creditors first and explain that you can't pay at the moment but you'll be back on track soon, you're showing yourself as more responsible than those who simply avoid their financial obligations. Your words will be music to their ears because they won't have to use a collection agency, which would only eat away at their profit.

It's hard to believe, but businesses dislike using collection agents even more than you dislike receiving their phone calls. After all, the collection agency gets to keep approximately one third of all the money it recovers from the customer. Not only that, but you the customer resent being chased down by a collection agent, despite your having brought on the matter yourself. A customer might harbor such resentment over the humiliation that they never want to do business with that company again. That's a double whammy for the company.

For those two reasons, businesses hate to sic collection agencies on people. Nevertheless, they are forced to do so every day because they cannot afford to let deadbeats get away with not paying their bills. Businesses recognize that it takes a lot of courage to call a creditor, so they'll repay the favor by helping you out.

Don't think for a moment that you are the first person to get behind on a financial obligation. It happens *all the time*. In America, a million people a year declare bankruptcy, a situation that basically allows people to completely renege on their financial promises. I don't believe in bankruptcy and don't recommend it in most situations. It's a little like dieting via liposuction: sure, they can suck out the fat, but unless we change our behavior, we're going to be back in the same bloated position we were in before we had the operation. For this and many other reasons, bankruptcy is not the best choice for most people.

However, paying our bills on time is, and so is talking with our creditors whenever we run into a problem. Virtually every company in business today has a policy of providing a month with a minimum payment—or even no payment—for anyone who gets into trouble. This is not the first time that they will have ever gotten a call like this. They're not going to say, "Ooooh, you *bad*. You didn't pay your bill. We gonna *fix* you." What they will say is something to the effect of "Would it be acceptable to make a minimum payment of $15 this month?" In other words, if you extend the courtesy of letting them know your situation, they in turn will be equally courteous and offer options to lighten your load. I have yet to hear of a creditor giving anyone a hard time when they explained honestly that they needed a little help.

If you want to earn a Medal of Honor, make the phone call in front of your high school–age kids. This act requires a certain amount of humility and courage that any child can admire. Parents don't need to be rich to earn their kids' respect. They need only be honest, straightforward, and brave.

STAY ON TRACK

The time has come to discuss the dreaded task of keeping financial records. Most people's financial "filing systems" get about as complicated as a shoebox. When the end of the year comes, they dump the shoebox on the tax preparer's desk and say, "Make sense out of this." I don't need to tell you that this is not a wise approach. Not only is it sloppy, but each of those pieces of paper will take time for your accountant to go through—and your accountant's time is directly proportional to the size of your final bill. There's a much simpler, more organized method that won't get you into hot financial water. In fact, it's so simple you can incorporate this approach into your family financial powwows.

Start off by buying a few file folders; eight or ten will do. File folders can be found in any office supply store, many stationery stores, and even some supermarkets. Label one of the files "Bills Paid." Every time you pay a bill, stick it in this folder. Label your second file folder "Bank." In this folder, keep your bank statements. Label your third file folder "Charitable." In this one, keep track of all the money that you donate to charitable organizations, whether it's cash you put in the Sunday collection plate or a check you write to a good cause. You may be able to take these amounts off your taxes. Your next file should be labeled "Income." In this file, include *all* of the pay stubs you receive over the course of a year, no matter how many jobs you work. The IRS only cares how much you were paid in total, so keep all those figures together. Label the next file folder "Medical." Here, put all the doctor bills, medical insurance copayments, and drug store receipts related to your family's medical care. These may also be deductible, depending on your tax situation. But since you cannot deduct what you cannot prove, you need to keep careful records of the medical expenses for every family member.

Label your last file "Taxes." In this file, keep any correspondence that you receive from the IRS. Believe it or not, the IRS is more interested in auditing lower-income people than they are in auditing the wealthy. Wealthy people may have more money, but they also have more lawyers and accountants who make it much harder to shake a few thousand dollars out of their clients. It's far easier to make a lower-income individual cough up a few hundred dollars. The IRS also figures, quite rightly, that one of their letters will scare you more than the guy in the Mercedes in Malibu. When a rich person receives a letter from the IRS, he just hands it off to his accountant, who takes care of it. If some extra tax truly is due, the rich guy writes a check and forgets all about it. So the IRS, in its great collective wisdom, has decided to come after you, the lower-income individual. You're much less likely to dispute a letter from the IRS saying you owe more money. Most lower-income individuals do not even consider that the IRS could have made a mistake.

In addition to the file folders already named, have some others on hand and visible. One should be labeled "Bills," and into it go the bills you have not yet paid. This folder will become another member at your family financial summits. Label another file folder "Call." This is where you put all documents that require a telephone call from you. Perhaps you have a question about a particular charge on your phone bill, like the mysterious two-hour call to Bora Bora. Set up a regular schedule for making such calls, perhaps the day after your family financial summits. Label another file "Write," and use it to hold any documents that require you to write a letter. On the last file, write "Deposit." Here you'll keep checks until you go to the bank. Strangely enough, some people don't view checks as being as valuable as cash. They're much more likely to lose a $500 check than a $1 bill. If this is you, I want you to know that your attitude would be completely different if you ever have to ask someone to write a new check to replace the one you've lost. So keep all the checks in this one folder, and then get them to the bank as soon as possible.

This filing system is simple, and kitchen-tested. I'm sure you will find, as have countless families already, that these simple tools will help you keep your documents and financial planning in check.

CHECKS AND BALANCING

Finally, we come to the much-awaited topic of balancing the checkbook. Let me guess: you've never balanced your checkbook. When your check statement arrives, you toss it in a drawer or, worse, throw it out. That's so *last week*. From now on, balancing the checkbook will become a part of your family financial summit.

Banking on Our Future

For those of you now sweating the idea of taking on this task, rest assured. It's not that hard to do. I'll give you the basics, and if you are still not entirely sure, you can consult your friendly bank officer, who will be happy to show you. Or come down to Operation HOPE, and one of our counselors will walk you through the process. The key reason for balancing your checkbook is that banks make mistakes. Often big mistakes. And never in your favor.

Balancing a checkbook is very simple. All it involves is looking to see which checks have cleared and which have not ("cleared" means that the check has been deducted from your account). Then look to see which deposits, if any, have not yet been credited to your account. Compare the amount on your statement, minus the checks that have not yet cleared and plus the deposits that have not yet been recorded, to the number in your checkbook (or on Quicken, if you're using it). If the number is radically different, you must go back and determine where the mistake was made—and whether the fault is the bank's or your own.

Banks are no longer surprised to have customers point out mistakes made on their account. Although you may think banks have a conspiracy going, I assure you that no bank would deliberately make mistakes with a person's account. The repercussions just aren't worth it. Not only would they risk federal punishment, but also they risk losing their good reputation—and, thus, their customers. However, honest human error often leads to mistakes that in turn end up on your bank statement.

Also, when you look at your bank statement, you'll see exactly how much you are being charged for such features as ATM usage. If you use an ATM from a bank other than your own, chances are that both banks have each charged you a separate fee, anywhere from $1.25 to $2. Let's say you take $20 out of an ATM. If both banks charge you $2, you just paid a 20 percent fee to access your money. Although the practice doesn't seem fair, banks do it all the time. The solution is to use ATMs less, and to make sure that you use only ATMs from your own bank. Some banks, such as Washington Mutual, never charge an ATM usage fee, even if they're not your bank. ATM fees are another feature to look into when you're opening your bank account.

Believe it or not, those are the basics of record keeping. Congratulate yourself on making it through! Now, teach your children these basics.

PART 2

Teaching Your Elementary Student about Money

CHAPTER 4

How to Talk about Money
with Your Kids

I think one key is to keep kids knowledgeable but not obsessed with money—to give them tools to manage their money but not be overconscious about it. I teach my kids that money is the means to an end, not the end. Money is the tool to achieve the goal, not the goal.

SUSAN KEATING, PARENT,

BANKING ON OUR FUTURE PARTICIPANT

Some parents say it's easier to talk about drugs or sex with their kids than to talk about money. In this chapter, we'll explore how to open up a dialogue with your kids about personal finances.

"The only lecture we listen to is the lecture we give ourselves." So says my mentor and spiritual advisor, the Reverend Dr. Cecil Murray of the First A.M.E. Church of Los Angeles, and I agree.

Nobody likes lectures. Your kids don't like you admonishing them about grades, their rooms, or their questionable "taste" in clothing. But if you look back far enough, you'll recall that you didn't enjoy being lectured, either. The way to inspire your kids is with the inspiration of enlightened self-interest.

Instead of lecturing, bring them into the discussion and allow their suggestions to be heard. Give them a voice in the family's fi-

nancial matters, and give them the responsibility of their own finances. By making family finances a group effort, you will be giving
your kids a hands-on opportunity to learn from experience—both
theirs and yours.

BE OPEN ABOUT FAMILY FINANCES

In the first part of this book, we discussed how you'll be writing
down your spending on that big pad of accountant ledger paper. Remember, don't be hiding that ledger paper away! Leave it out in the
kitchen, where everyone sees it every single day. Let your kids see
where the money goes.

Most children, rich or poor, have absolutely no concept of what
it costs to live. They don't know how large a rent or mortgage payment can be, or even the cost of putting groceries on the table.
They can't yet comprehend the effort you put into bringing home
the bacon, or even what a pound of bacon might cost. Their knowledge of the cost of clothing consists mainly of that "phat" $100 pair
of shoes they covet at the mall.

I advocate financial transparency. This means that your kids
should be able to look in and see exactly where your money goes.
Okay, maybe you don't want to let them know absolutely everything. But by and large, why shouldn't your kids know what life
costs? It can be quite a sobering realization for kids to see just how
expensive life is. If anything, your kids will respect you even more
when they see how hard you work and how quickly money disap-
pears on basic necessities—food, clothing, and shelter. They'll also
see that because you are spending wisely, you are able to save and
pay off any credit card debt you may have incurred.

No parental lecture has the power inherent in parental example.
If your kids regularly see bounced checks coming back from the
bank, they'll have a hard time taking anything you say seriously. If
you are financially responsible, your kids will look to you as a role
model. And if you are less than financially responsible, they will
only be too delighted to follow your example! Let's provide great ex-

amples for our kids, because one great example is worth a thousand nagging words.

NOW IT'S THEIR TURN

My second suggestion is to give each of your kids, elementary age and up, accountant ledgers and have them come up with their own categories and items. These might include clothing, entertainment, music, and whatever else your kids are into. Ask them to keep track of their own spending, and maybe give them some kind of reward, financial or otherwise, for every week when they have kept track of their numbers. Give them something that will motivate them to keep on track, even if it's as simple as a day off from chores. Make it into a game or competition if you have more than one child, especially when they're young. Give them the idea that keeping track of their money can be fun.

My friend Jennie introduced me to the Star Chart, an idea her aunt came up with after one too many fights over which cousin's turn it was to vacuum. Her Aunt Marilyn drew up a list of chores that Jennie and her cousin Brietta routinely neglected to perform around the house. Next to each chore, she put a value—one star, two stars, three stars—with the most despised chores (vacuuming, cleaning the litter box, and so on) receiving the highest star value. After completing a task, Jennie and Brietta would receive the appropriate amount of stars. They would then anxiously look at the bottom of the Star Chart—which acted as a scoreboard of the cousins' participation—and look at the "star exchange rate," the amount of actual money each earned star was worth. Let's say that five stars equaled one dollar. Once a month, the cousins were allowed to cash in their "stars," so if they had earned 20 up to that point, they had $4 to spend.

While this may sound like outright bribery (or, at the very least, a legal system of child labor), Jennie told me that the Star Chart taught her much more than the simple math involved in converting tin foil stars for cash (which may be the root of her interest in foreign currencies and exchange rates). Not only did the system encourage her to help around the house with less complaining, but also it taught her how to save up for that once-a-month spending spree. Jennie quickly learned that if she used all the stars she had accumulated in a given month (about 35), there was no way she'd be able to buy the coveted dome tent (worth roughly the equivalent of 85 stars!) she'd been eyeing. Instead of spending all her stars, Jennie would buy one or two five-star items, letting the rest of her stars ride until the next month. In three months, she had her tent — as well as a newfound respect for saving and patience. Twenty years later, Jennie told me, she still has that tent. "It was the first item I ever really *earned*," she says with pride.

But the kids weren't the only ones to reap benefits. Her Aunt Marilyn was pleased when she realized that with her system the cousins were fighting over who was going to vacuum — except now they both *wanted* to! The five stars allocated to each room of the house was too much for either of them to pass up. What's more, Marilyn no longer had to ask the girls to do chores. As a matter of fact, she had to explain that vacuuming the living room twice in two hours did not earn 10 stars. Not only did Marilyn have the cleanest house on the block, she no longer had two preteen girls complaining of nothing to do. And, rather than having a set allowance, the girls were learning how they could control their income by the level of effort they put in.

MORE ABOUT THE FAMILY FINANCIAL SUMMITS

Discuss money with your kids, elementary age and up, on a regular basis by holding family financial summits. Whether you decide to do this weekly or monthly, make sure that you keep to a schedule, such as after dinner the first Sunday of the month. Mark the date on a calendar where everyone in the family can see it. At the summit, go over your spending with your kids, and take a look at what they've written down on their accounting sheets as well. Explain why you are spending money the way you are. Make family finances a true family-wide occupation. Allow your kids to offer suggestions. They might realize they're buying certain nonessential items that they can do without. Maybe they would rather have other things.

Most important, let them know how you are doing in terms of saving. For most families, sharing this information will constitute an absolute revolution. Most parents, rich or poor, never tell their kids a thing about money, let alone the money they save for rainy days. Explain what short- and long-term savings are for. Maybe one savings plan is for short-term objectives, such as a trip to the zoo or a family camera. Long-term savings might include a vacation or a college fund. Your kids will see the importance of long-term goals as each short-term goal is reached. After finally having the funds for a trip to the amusement park, they'll see that the long-term goals will also be realized one day.

You may also give them the option of keeping the family finances a private matter not to be discussed with their friends or letting them share the fact that they are involved in the family spending decisions. Who knows? You might start influencing other families in your community to become more financially aware.

In any event, make your family financial summits fun and upbeat. Ask for your kids' opinions, and really listen to them. They just might surprise you with their suggestions, and you'll soon begin to see how their financial knowledge is growing.

Ensure that everyone takes part in the summits by setting an attendance rule. Schedule the meetings at a time when all the kids will be home. If conflicting schedules make that impossible, meet with each child individually on a regular basis. Your kids need to know that nothing comes ahead of taking care of their finances — not sports, after-school jobs, or girlfriends or boyfriends. Make this rule nonnegotiable. Whatever time you set aside is sacred for your family to discuss this most important issue. A solid financial future is something no one can afford to miss!

When you do have your family financial summits, make sure to eliminate all distractions. Turn off the TV and stereo, and turn on the answering machine so that a phone call won't interrupt you. Sit around the table with your family, and work through the numbers.

Financial literacy is one of the most important gifts you could possibly give your children. They may not understand exactly how valuable it is now, but when they hit the real world and have to be financially self-sufficient themselves, they will have a huge advantage over their peers, whether they're from the nicest suburbs or the meanest streets of the inner city.

SET GOALS

Teach your children to have financial goals. When kids know what they want, they are often willing to work hard to achieve it—as evidenced by Jennie's patience in saving up stars for her prized tent. You might want to suggest to your elementary school–age children that they save a certain percentage of their allowance, cash gifts from relatives, or any other money they receive (say, when a savings bond comes due). Half to toys? Sure. As long as half gets put away for the future.

How can young children set financial goals? The same way adults do. Have your kids make lists of the toys, games, or articles of clothing they want. Ask them to find out what those items cost, either in stores or (with your guidance) on the Internet. Teach them to prioritize their goals by deciding which items they want most. Then, help them create a special fund, which you can keep for them in an envelope, out of their reach.

You could also offer to match what they save with a contribution of your own, just as corporations sometimes match employees' donations to retirement accounts. Your kids will be encouraged to save money instead of immediately spending it, and they will learn how saving money can help them achieve their goals.

If you instill these habits early, the dividends will pay off later. Let's look ahead just for a moment and see how starting your kids on goal setting at an early age can make a huge difference as they reach middle school and high school. Ask your older kids what sort of financial goals, both short- and long-term, they would like to set for themselves. Have them write down where they see themselves in six months, a year, after college, and five years after that. Then analyze with them exactly how they can achieve these goals. Chances are, their goals will not be achievable by earning $8 an hour in an after-school job. Kids need to be shown that immediate gratification, if left unchecked, can stall their hopes of long-term financial success. Show your kids that it's not just about working harder—it's about working *smarter*.

Encourage your kids to have big goals. It is far too easy to break the spirits of our children by discouraging them from setting significant goals for themselves. Allowing children to dream and accomplish only a portion of a goal is better than telling them to dream small to avoid disappointment.

Teaching children to avoid disappointment by setting low goals trains them to accept a lifetime filled with frustration and dissatisfaction. We need to teach our kids to aim high. Show them how to set up small goals to help them obtain a larger goal. Explain how to do this on a daily basis. For example, a small (relatively), short-term goal may be to ace an upcoming math exam. The grade your daughter receives helps her achieve the larger goal of an overall "A" in math for the quarter. That overall math grade, in turn, affects her GPA (grade point average), which is one of the application factors colleges consider. While that one math test won't determine whether your daughter gets into Yale, it is a step—however small— in the process.

Discuss your children's goals at your family financial summits.

The key to communicating finances with kids is to have discussions based on your honest financial situation, as opposed to lectures and shouting matches. When you give your time and wisdom to your kids on a regular basis, they are bound to repay that effort by becoming more financially literate themselves. You'll find that you now have common ground with your kids in a way that you might never have thought possible. Involve your children in your financial life so that they can learn for themselves how best to handle their own money.

CHAPTER 5

A Penny Saved . . .

As children, my older sister and I sold Christmas cards every year to earn
money for gifts or to earn prizes that we wanted for Christmas. We built
quite a lucrative business, which resulted in our mother not needing to
spend a lot of money for our Christmas presents. In addition, she insisted
that we save some of the money to add to our savings accounts. I was always
interested in how money works. My mother began allowing me to help her
balance her checking account when I was in the sixth grade, and in subse-
quent years, that became one of my tasks that I thoroughly enjoyed.

FRANCES JAMES, BANKING ON
OUR FUTURE OUTREACH CONSULTANT

No child is too young to learn that the key to success in life
is knowing how to save the money you make.
Start off as early as kindergarten by buying your child a piggy
bank. Today such banks come in all shapes, sizes, and colors. Make
the process of saving even more fun by purchasing a bank that ap-
peals to your child's particular interests. We can treat money like a
burden, or we can wear our financial lives in hip-hop style—loose
and free—and have fun. I believe in hard work, but I also believe in
fun! Make it fun for your child to be a smart, happy saver.
Your family financial summit is the perfect time to explore what

A Penny Saved . . .

a savings account is all about. Even your kids can open a no-fee savings account . . . for just $5 (we'll get to that in the next chapter). Help your children understand what banks do, because banks play such an important part in all of our financial lives.

MAKE FINANCE FUN

Remember: the key is to make it fun. Before your family financial summit, you may want to plan a field trip to the bank with your children. Although television has familiarized most children with the large vaults and other security measures found in financial institutions, seeing how these work in person can have a tremendous effect. If you have a safe deposit box, access it that day to show them both how you protect your valuables and how the security measures at the bank work. Make a deposit or withdrawal with a teller so that they see how they can access their money whenever they want.

At the next summit, have your children bring a bunch of toys — dolls, baseball cards, stuffed animals. Give each of those toys some Monopoly money, and choose an object (such as a shoebox) to act as a bank. Your kids are now going to become knowledgeable about the banking system.

Explain that it's not wise to keep all of our money in the house. First of all, we might lose it, or it might be lost through no fault of our own — a fire, a robbery, or even an accidental swish of the vacuum. Make clear that money left around the house can sometimes disappear.

Describe the concept of interest. Tell them that the bank will actually *pay them* for holding their money over a period of time. Although the amount may not be a lot, it's certainly more than what your house would pay them! Then let each of your children's toys act as depositors in the "bank." Show your child that if a teddy bear puts $100 of Monopoly money into the bank, at the end of the year the bank gives Teddy the original $100 back — plus another $5. Show your children that the money is safe in the bank, and remind them of the security measures you saw during your field trip.

Banking on Our Future

If your children are older, explain that a government entity called the Federal Deposit Insurance Corporation guarantees the safety of any money you put in the bank. If robbers come and steal money from the bank, the FDIC will give you back every dollar that you put in. (Unless your child's lemonade stand is about to be franchised, you don't need to mention that the cap is $100,000.) If the bank burns down, the FDIC will make sure that Teddy gets back his money. If your children are a little older, you can go into more detail about banks and the FDIC. For those of you who need to brush up on your facts, here's some basic information to get you by.

THE FDIC AND YOU

Dating back to the earliest days of U.S. history, the traditional savings account has always played an important role in our banking and economic systems. Savings and real estate ownership were two of the first forms of investment and equity accumulation in this country. That is, people have been making money by owning real estate since America began.

Banks, insured since after the Great Depression by the full faith and credit of the federal government, take in deposits—the very lifeblood of banks—and pay a modest rate of interest to depositors. Based on my personal experience, I have found that the rate of interest paid on savings accounts is at or just above the rate of inflation. Credit unions often offer more competitive rates, so be sure to check which ones you're qualified to join, and compare their rates to those of local banks.

While there have been several funds and structures for insuring banking deposits over the past sixty-plus years, today those deposits are insured by the FDIC, the federal agency that serves both as an insurer of depository funds and a regulator of bank activity. The FDIC is the only federal banking regulator that has mandated regulatory authority over all banks licensed and operating in the United States. Likewise, banks are among the rare breed of quasi-public, quasi-private entities that enjoy the benefit of a preferred relationship with the U.S. federal government.

It is the banks' job to put that savings capital—your and my individual savings accounts on deposit—to work for the benefit of the bank and its shareholders. To perform this duty, banks take those same deposits, which might pay 3 percent annual interest, add on 2 to 3 percent for overhead costs and another 2 to 3 percent in "profit," and lend the funds out to consumer and commercial borrowers for a wide range of needs. This means, in this example, that the banks' "benchmark lending rate" to borrowers must be in the 7 to 9 percent range.

While this may sound like banks are making money hand over fist, the reality is quite different. It is true that, as a result of banks having to put up capital of only 8 to 10 percent while the public provides the remaining 90 to 92 percent of every dollar lent, banks have an incredible opportunity for leverage. That is part of the reason that banks are one of the oldest industries in America today. But there is not much room for error in banking, and banks will eat through their 2 percent profit margin and quickly begin to lose money if they are not making solid credit decisions. This said, the savings account holder is always covered against loss, as long as they stay within the $100,000 maximum deposit limit. Bank savings accounts are both the most conservative form of "investment," and the lowest yielding.

Much of this information will be over the heads of little ones. That's okay. This information is really for you and your older children. Let's get back to the school-age kids who are now becoming bank depositors.

FURTHER FUN WITH FINANCE

Your kids may wonder how banks are able to "give away" money—that is, pay interest. If they're not yet old enough to grasp the concept of loans and investments, you can simply tell them that's what banks do. That's what makes them "interesting." However, if they don't buy your game, you can enlist Teddy and Barbie in some further role-playing.

Show your kids that Teddy's money doesn't just sit in a big pile in a safe. Barbie is also a bank customer, and she wants to open up a clothing store. The bank will study Barbie to see if her clothing store is a good idea and if she's a good, honest businessperson. The bank will look at Barbie's history with the bank and note if she's always paid her bills, made regular mortgage payments on the Dream House, and loaned money to Ken in a sensible manner. If Barbie checks out, the bank will take some of the money from the depositors (open up the "bank," and take out a handful of cash) and lend it to Barbie to open her clothing store. You might show Skipper buying a new skirt from Barbie's store.

Then you can show your children that Barbie will pay back to the bank the money that she borrowed to open her store. Explain that Barbie actually pays the bank a little more than she borrowed—her interest on her loan. Tell your kids that this additional money is where their interest comes from, as well as the money that the bank makes as profit for itself and to pay its employees.

You can tailor this lesson to the age and attention span of your children. You can also have it go on for some time, as some of the other toys decide to start their own companies and borrow money from the bank. Have Ken deposit money every week, since he is saving 10 percent of his income like a responsible toy. Show your kids that money has a life of its own and that when it's out there working for us, we can make even more money.

Many board games also illustrate the big picture of banks and financial decisions, Monopoly being the most popular. Check with your local toy store and see what games they have that are appropriate for your children's age groups. You can make your family financial summits more fun by closing the meeting with a game or two. While playing, explain to your kids why you are making your decisions so that they understand the thought process that goes into spending, saving, and investing.

A Penny Saved . . .

Most kids think that the only thing you can do with money is spend it.

Here, you will be giving them a graphic, fun illustration of the fact that an alternative to spending money is saving money—and that the reward of saving money is that you get even more money as a result. You might have Snoopy saving up to buy a nice doghouse, or Kermit saving up for a new lily pad. The goal is to convey to your children, as early in their lives as possible, the idea that money does not have to burn a hole in their pockets. There are alternatives to the mall when it comes to deciding just where they want to put their allowance or the money they earn at part-time jobs.

Make sure to have fun with your illustration of the banking system. It may well be that your children enjoy it so much that they want to play bank again and again, or by themselves. Let them! Once again, you are giving them an advantage in life that will always pay rich dividends.

CHAPTER 6

How to Open Your Own No-Fee Savings Account with Just $5

I feel that teaching children about fiscal responsibility early on in life helps to set up a strong foundation about how to handle money as an adult. I remember when I was in third grade, my mother and grandmother helped me open a Christmas Club account at the bank. I used to put in at least $.25 a week from my allowance into the Christmas Club. When Christmas came around, I had saved $25. The presents I bought for my family were not big, but I was so proud that they were from money that I had saved. The examples my family gave me early on have helped me to appreciate the value of money and how to budget wisely.

ROSE TOYAMA, KINDERGARTEN MENTOR TEACHER

In our last chapter, we learned to teach our kids to have fun playing make-believe with banks. Now it's time to transform that make-believe into reality.

It takes a lot less than you and your kids might think to open up a savings account. How about . . . $5! That's about five Snickers bars. In this chapter, you'll learn how your kids can open up a savings account with just a $5 bill.

I have been doing so much with so little for so long, I can do almost anything with nothing.

I have used this axiom in business for years, to grow my various enterprises from almost nothing to a little bit of something special. This savvy financial theory came not from business school or business experience but from my youth. I saw my father stretch and leverage a dollar in his business. My sister, brother, and I used to joke that our mother was so thrifty that she could rub the buffalo off a nickel.

My parents' approach to savings and investment was simple: it's not what you make, it's what you keep that's important. You cannot start saving early enough. No amount of money is too little to begin saving with. The habit of saving is what's most important.

START-UP PROGRAMS FOR YOUTHS

When I was growing up, bankers would come into the classroom and teach economic education. Some banks would allow you to open a small savings account. Those times came and went. Why those banks stopped banking on *our* future, I'll never know.

Operation HOPE's Banking on Our Future program, along with several leading banks and financial service companies around the country, has started teaching economic literacy in classrooms again. For all youth completing these programs, with the approval of parents and guardians, banks are now beginning to open starter savings accounts with an opening balance of as little as $5. Check with your local bank to see if such a program exists. If not, call us at Operation HOPE—and we'll be happy to talk with the bank and explain the virtues of the program!

One bank-sponsored program provides young people who complete a participating economic literacy program with $5 to $25 starter savings account vouchers. These vouchers can then be taken to a neighborhood bank branch, redeemed for a comparable value of U.S. currency, and deposited into a new starter savings account.

Another unique program in the late 1990s was sponsored by Bank of America in Atlanta, Georgia. The bank built miniature youth bank branches inside black churches, offering, among other things, $5 starter savings accounts to youth maintaining a minimum grade point average. Bank of America generated more than $300,000 in youth deposits from eighteen youth banking locations!

It doesn't matter how much money you and your children have in a savings account or other form of investment. What matters is that kids get in the habit of saving, and it's important to learn how banks can help kids save.

CREATE A LIFELONG MEMORY

Take your children down to the local bank and open up savings accounts for them. This excursion is the sort of experience that no child will ever forget. Your taking time out of your busy day to help them get their own financial start is something they will remember for the rest of their lives. One day, when they are older, they will take their own children to the bank to open up starter savings accounts for them, and they will look back on that memorable day when you did the same for them.

One credit card company's ad campaign on television talks about how the best experiences you can offer your children are priceless. Well, for a mere $5, you can help your child open a savings account—and give them a memory they will never forget.

PART 3

Financial Literacy for Middle School Kids

CHAPTER 7

Corporate America
Wants Your Kid's Body

I was teaching a Banking on Our Future class to thirty high school students about credit. My first question was "How many of you have received a credit application?" About half of the class raised their hands. My second question was "What did you do with them?" To my surprise, the answer was "We ripped them up." My third question was "Why did you do that?" They answered, "Because we don't need them." The good news about all of that was that they had listened and were putting what they learned into practice. The challenge is to spread the word.

BILL BECKER, BANKING ON OUR FUTURE
BANKER-TEACHER VOLUNTEER IN LOS ANGELES

You may think your middle school child is too young for credit cards, but that's not how businesses think. Believe it or not, your eleven-year-old is already being targeted as a potential future credit card debtor.

Innocent-sounding points programs are becoming increasingly popular among kids' favorite brands. Chances are your kids are already earning "Coke Cash" or "Pepsi Points." These seemingly practical and fun programs are actually a backdoor way to get kids hooked on the idea of credit cards, affinity programs (where dollars spent earn points for other goods or services), and brand loyalty.

To put it bluntly, our children are getting pimped, as are inner-city and low- to moderate-income communities. Corporate America has found an almost limitless profit center in the appetite of the youth market, and some are riding it for all it's worth.

This said, no one can "pimp" you unless you let them. When thirteen-year-olds are buying gum and toys and college students are paying for pizza with their newest credit card — *in their own name* — simply because they do not have the cash, you can blame corporate America, which is winning the battle but losing the war.

In this case, the "battle" is to make money in the short term. The "war," if you will, is the creation of a new generation of consumers who will shop responsibly instead of destroying themselves financially. Corporate America is helping to raise a generation of financial incompetents. The culture it's promoting causes young people financial ruin and cultural maladjustment before they are old and mature enough to become real, long-term customers, clients, and borrowers.

Did you know that when your kids sign up for affinity programs, they give out their e-mail addresses to major corporations? Do you really want your kids to be getting mail from Pepsi? Don't you have a hard enough time keeping your children's diet healthy without a major producer of junk food — laden with sugar, caffeine, and chemicals — competing with you for their attention?

The lengths to which companies go in order to establish a sense of brand loyalty with your kids is astonishing. Here's what your kids will get if they register with MountainDew.com:

At MountainDew.com, kids have access to a variety of activities that focus on Mountain Dew and its products including music, games and Mountain Dew–sponsored athletes. The content really runs the gamut: They can play Shockwave games like our "Skate" game, listen to music from our online radio station, "Radio Free Dew," download

screensavers and "wallpaper" for their computer and much more. Plus,
they'll have chances to win prizes from our contests and sign up to re-
ceive our online newsletter.

Do you really want your kids to be "Doing the Dew" every time
they check their e-mail? When you're trying to educate your kids
about the importance of delayed gratification, do you really want
to compete with Niketown's e-mails about their new $160 Air
FlightPosite III basketball shoes?

Sit down with your children and find out exactly which websites
they've registered with. You might be shocked to discover just how
much direct contact these companies have with your kids—without any supervision or guidance from you.

Do you really want your child's name, address, and *age* on a database? Sure, the companies all *promise* never to disclose information
to third parties, but any hacker worth his or her salt can gain access
to a corporation's computer files at any time. What's more, recent
lawsuits have attempted to classify client mailing lists as assets,
meaning that should the company be sold, their database of names
transfers ownership to the highest bidder.

Corporate America is courting today's youth as it has no generation before. Why now? For a host of reasons, this generation has
access to more disposable cash and income than any previous generation. To make matters worse, direct advertising has never been
easier or more affordable.

BRANDED BY LOYALTY

Corporate America has done a remarkable job of marketing to a
generation hooked on brand identities. It is our responsibility as
parents to make every effort to inform our children that they are being manipulated and economically stripped. Young people hate
being controlled, by anyone or anything. If we educate youth and
let them make their own decisions, their disdain for authority will
save them—without the lectures they resent and ignore anyway.

Banking on Our Future

Despite what they may say, children look to adults for guidance, but usually in the form of example. Your kids are watching you. Take a look at your own wardrobe and ask yourself how many of your clothes display a visible label indicating the manufacturer's or designer's name. When I see kids wearing Tommy Hilfiger's name emblazoned across their chests, two questions pop into my mind: How much is Tommy Hilfiger paying these kids to become human billboards? And whose name does Tommy Hilfiger have on his chest? You already know the answers.

People used to buy brand names simply because a brand name could be trusted. In earlier times, when so much shoddy merchandise made it to the marketplace, you wanted brand names on anything you bought so that you could make sure you were not buying junk. That is no longer the case. So many high-quality goods sell for limited prices that it's hard to dump junk on sophisticated American consumers. We don't need brand names to tell us that a sneaker or deodorant is good. Virtually everything you can buy in any respectable store is high quality.

Today, brand names perform a different, rather sad function. They provide a facade of self-esteem for young people, especially those in urban areas. Kids derive a sense of belonging by flaunting Calvin Klein's name on their clothes, drinking a certain brand of bottled water, or even wearing a car's hood emblem around their neck. For them, brands offer an "in" to the exclusive clubs they see advertised on TV. They believe the hype that if Brandy wears Maybelline, they should too. They become convinced that they can't be cool unless they're wearing Air Nikes advertised by Michael Jordan. Wearing a shirt with a polo player embroidered on the front gives them the same sense of belonging as a college student who proudly wears his fraternity letters. They let their clothing speak for them by associating their identity with others wearing the same threads.

This kind of ostentatious consumerism is not as harmful to people who can afford it. But in the 'hood, these brand names are literally killing us. In the 1980s and early 1990s we heard tragic stories of young children being gunned down so someone could steal their brand-name sneakers. Brand names are killing us financially as well. Buying brand-name items is an inner-city addiction as much as a suburban one—and it's become almost as costly as heroin.

MODEL BEHAVIOR

There is no easy way to get your kids off brand names and the compulsion to buy items with big, visible labels. The best you can do is be a good role model and limit the amount of blatant brand-name items you purchase. Let your kids see that it's possible to be a happy, well-adjusted adult without Donna Karan's name or Nike's logo splayed all over your body. Again, teach the lesson by *being* the lesson.

If your kids won't take a lesson from you, perhaps they'll listen to one of their idols. When you're watching television, point out what a "dope" shirt Sarah Michelle Gellar is wearing, then comment that you never see *her* with some logo splashed across her body. Point out that some of the clothes on these shows are "vintage" (a word that carries much more cachet than the dreaded "second-hand"), and tell them how you'd never find a truly choice piece of antique clothing on Macy's racks. If you point out how each of their favorite stars has developed their own style, rather than simply mimicking their Hollywood brethren, you might influence them to strike out on their own and build a wardrobe based on their personal tastes.

If you have younger children, find a fashion magazine and cut out the pictures of the celebrities—then cut their heads off. Most celebrities have a distinct style that is readily recognizable to even the elementary school set. Have your children try to guess whose head belongs to each body. Help them along with ridiculous statements like "Wow, these ripped jeans look *so* Cher" or "Doesn't this gold chain look like something Will Smith would wear?" They'll know better and set you straight. When they've correctly matched everyone up, point out how Janet Jackson wouldn't be caught dead in Salma Hayek's outfit—it's just not *her*. Even though the outfits are pricey and over-the-top, your kids will see that celebrities create their own style rather than copy someone else's outfit. Stress how each one looks good in the ensemble of their choice.

Even if you don't succeed in breaking your children's brand-name obsession, you might be able to hit them where it hurts most: the wallet. If your daughter has been pestering you for that $250 suede jacket she's just *got* to have, point out the various other items she could buy with the same money. "If you get that jacket, then I guess you don't want that shirt, those shoes, and the five sweaters you pointed out last time we were at the mall." Or find a similar-looking item for less and show them that, had they not bought a brand name, they could have bought *two* for the price of the one designer garment. Show them that their choices have repercussions on their future spending and you'll gain more credibility than if you simply lectured them on the evils of brand names.

If the clothing selection *du jour* in your kids' schools involves brand-name goods, as is most likely the case, good luck. You're facing an uphill fight. While you may not be able to break your children's addiction to items that carry a larger price tag simply because of the name on the label, you might be able to make a bit of a difference in their thinking for later on. As parents, we frequently have to act like a broken record, repeating the same message until kids finally hear—and listen. No one changes overnight. Nonetheless, just because the battle is not easy to win doesn't mean we shouldn't fight it. Get out there and do the best you can. Teach your kids that they don't need to spend their money and serve as free advertising—or, in some neighborhoods, risk their lives—in order to be accepted. In a crazy world, parents have to be a beacon of sanity. Otherwise, we are forfeiting our responsibilities as role models and shapers of the future.

Intervene early because teenagers are the single most desirable demographic group in the whole country. They have more money to spend as they please than any other age group. They have yet to make decisions about which toothpaste, laundry detergent, or shampoo they'll buy for the rest of their lives. These two factors

Corporate America Wants Your Kid's Body

alone are enough to make corporations covet kids—from head to toe. Businesses spend billions of dollars annually to influence buying decisions and to coax hard-earned dollars from their pockets. If you think they have your kids' best interests at heart, then think again.

THE INSECURITIES MARKET

The one character trait of practically every adolescent and teenager, from the barrio to Beverly Hills, is insecurity. Teens are among the least secure people on earth. They are terrified of doing anything that might cause them to be ostracized by their peers.

Confidence cannot be bought in the store, nor can it be taught in a class. You cannot give kids a magic pill called confidence. Instead, confidence must be developed over a long period of time.

People who have enjoyed longtime success are confident of their abilities. A bricklayer who has worked for fifteen years is confident of his ability to build a house. A fashion designer who has developed several hot clothing designs has confidence in her ability to set trends. Teenagers have not yet had the opportunity to hone their skills, social or otherwise, and thus lack the confidence required to stand tall among their peers.

Teenagers might appear bold or sassy. But the majority are covering up for a deep-seated feeling of uncertainty, if not outright inferiority. This lack of security is especially true for many children from low-income homes and children of color. They are perhaps even more full of doubt about themselves than their middle-class Caucasian counterparts. This is a fact of life that we who are raising black and Latino children must face.

So how do kids try to develop a sense of confidence? The same way adults do: they try to buy it. People who lack confidence are natural targets for marketers.

Here's a little-known fact: *every single ad geared at preteens and teens is created to remind them of their insecurities.*

An advertisement doesn't simply call your attention to a product's existence. Its real purpose is to create a sense of anxiety that the product is essential to your happiness. If you don't drink Pepsi, people will not like you. Without Calvin Klein's jeans, your sex life will be nonexistent. If you don't use Herbal Essences shampoo, no one will want to travel in your car with you. The point of every ad is to create a sense of panic that what you have, what you look like, what you drive, and even how you smell just isn't good enough.

Adults are able to ignore many of these messages because we've already made a lot of our basic brand-loyalty decisions. How many adults change toothpaste brands more than a couple of times after age twenty? How many adults try a dozen different shampoos to figure out which one is best for their hair? We buy either what's on sale or the brand we've become accustomed to. There's not much point in marketing to adults.

That's where your kids come into the mix. Because kids are still choosing, still desperately wanting to fit in, the message in every ad is simple: buying this product will boost your street worth and your self-esteem.

Marketers play on sexual confidence in particular. Notice how sex is used to sell nearly every product, from soup to Nissan Sentras. Advertisers use sex to sell products because sex gets our attention. A beautiful model, female or male, using a product causes people to sit up and pay attention more than the product alone could ever do. The image of the model is often much bigger than the picture of the product! Everybody enjoys looking at attractive people. If an advertiser can get you to associate the way you feel about sex with the way you feel about their underarm deodorant, you'll be more inclined to get a little tingle when you see their product on the shelf. If you don't think advertisers are selling sex to kids, just look at Christina Aguilera in that hot little outfit shaking it for Pepsi. How many thirty-five-year-old women do you think she is influencing to go out and drink a can of Pepsi? Not many. How many fifteen-year-old-boys is she lining up to take the Pepsi challenge? You can't count them all.

Corporate America Wants Your Kid's Body

Marketers use sex in advertising for another reason, and as a parent, you should be aware of it. Advertisers convey the idea that their product comes complete with a fantastic sex life, even in the ads they gear toward young people. See for yourself. Watch a television show pitched to kids. Choose one of your own kids' favorites. Then, during the commercial breaks, study the ads carefully. Ask yourself, What sense of insecurity is this ad trying to induce in my kids? Then ask yourself how the product claims to solve that insecurity. You probably won't believe ads work this way until you sit down and scrutinize them.

Of course, no product can solve that problem for a kid—or an adult. And we're just as susceptible at times. After you've done your commercial-studying homework, ask yourself the ultimate question: *why would I want my child to have a better sex life?* If you're like most parents, you don't want your child to have any sex life at all. I have yet to meet a parent who was pleased to tell me that their teenager enjoys a better sex life than most married people. Never happened, never will happen. Advertisers are selling your children on the idea to have sex as early and with as many people as possible.

Once you've studied the ads, sit down with your kids and watch the ads. Explain to them what you now know—ads foster insecurity and promote sexual activity. Kids are not stupid. On the contrary, they are very astute. When they start to study ads, they will be amazed. They will be alive to the tricks of the advertisers. Will they succumb nevertheless? Perhaps. But certainly not to the same degree that they would have if you hadn't spoken with them.

Corporate America wants your kids' bodies *and* minds. Only one thing stands between advertisers and your kids: the truth. Share it with your kids. You'll all reap the benefits.

ATTACKING THE POVERTY OF THE SPIRIT

- "If I don't like me, I cannot like you."
- "If I don't respect me, I am not going to respect you."

- "If I don't feel good about me, I am not going to feel good about you."
- "If I don't have a meaningful purpose in my life, I am going to turn your life into a living hell."

I believe these four statements are why almost every inner-city community in America remains in a constant state of crisis. They are also why our children—and, truth be told, we too—cannot break out of the cycle of "He's got one, I want one too." One prominent author referred to it as poverty consciousness.

The War on Poverty failed in part because we attacked the wrong enemy. The real enemy is not things, buildings, or money, but ourselves. The poverty we must overcome is a poverty of the mind, body, and spirit, because the bottom line is that we simply do not feel good about ourselves. We could equip our children with all the best tools and financial planning skills available, but if we don't also pass down to our youth a high self-esteem, we are merely "re-arranging the deck chairs on the Titanic."

At Operation HOPE we focus our empowerment not on helping our clients "make more money" but on helping them "make better decisions with the money they make." The rich keep getting richer not because of what they make, but because of what they manage to keep!

Poverty consciousness says, "I need, I need." Your stability is always pulled, shoved, and ultimately manhandled by your appetite —your emotional appetite. In order to take control of your life, *you* have to control *you*, or your kids will never pay attention.

CHAPTER 8

Will You Take a Check?

All students need to have the tools of improvement in order to make informed choices about their financial future. As a child, I was given a weekly allowance that I used to purchase food and toys that I wanted. However, as an incentive to save my money, my father opened a savings account for me. He would match any funds that I deposited into my savings account. This resulted in a savings of over $5,000 by the time I graduated from high school. This was a very powerful lesson for me to encourage my savings. Additionally, the fact that the bank was within walking distance from my home encouraged me to make deposits even as small as $1.

KATHERINE NELSON, BANKING ON OUR FUTURE
INSTRUCTIONAL COORDINATOR

Adolescents open checking accounts for two reasons. Some do so in order to develop a sense of financial self-sufficiency and responsibility, and I applaud them. Your kids will be on the right financial track once they grasp the importance of checking accounts and the knowledge of how to open and maintain them.

The second reason adolescents open checking accounts is so sad and crazy that I would laugh if it didn't bring me to tears: their parents have messed up their own financial lives and can no longer get a checking account or a credit card, so they have their kids open up accounts in their place. And we wonder how our children end up in debt as adults. The fruit never falls far from the tree.

Let's talk about checking accounts. I hope you have a comfortable place to sit because it's going to be a *looooooong* chapter.

I CAN'T BE OVERDRAWN— I STILL HAVE SOME CHECKS!

The way some people handle their checking account leaves me dying with laughter. Why laughter? Because I have to laugh to keep from crying!

Many people use their checking account *exactly as they would a credit card*. They pay by check, praying the cashier doesn't see their fingers crossed in hopes there's enough money in their account. Or they write a check and put money in the account *later on* to cover the amount. If you're scratching your head wondering *why* this is crazy, then this chapter is dedicated to you. You need to understand exactly what a checking account is for before you can properly educate your children about how and why to use one.

People want to keep their money in a safe place, but they also want to have convenient access to it. Banks offer checking accounts so that their customers have easy access to their money without carrying around large amounts of cash. Most checking accounts offer the use of a checkbook and a debit card, which resembles a credit card and functions in much the same way. Debit cards also give customers access to their money via ATMs outside of regular banking business hours. Once a checking account is opened, a checkbook and a debit card allow customers to accomplish most banking needs without ever having to go inside a bank.

Ask your kids what a check is, and I think you'll find their answers very interesting. One child at a Banking on Our Future session said, "A check is what you pay someone with when you don't have any *real* money and you just want them to go away." The bottom line is that a check is nothing more than a promise to pay—an absolute promise to pay with "good funds" *you already have* in the bank. In reality, you don't even need a bank-issued piece of paper to make a purchase with a "check." Believe it or not, you could write your name, account number, bank routing number, the amount, the date, and your signature on the back of your T-shirt and take it to a local bank. While you may get the once-over, some delay, and more than a few quizzical looks, the bank *will* cash your shirt. A check can take almost any form as long as it has the account number, the bank routing number, the signature, and, of course, the amount.

CONVENIENCE? CHECK!

In banking terms, a checking account is "a convenience account designed for the orderly clearing of good funds." That's a fancy way of saying that you put money in the bank and you can take it out, one check at a time. With a checking account, you can even wire funds in and out of your account. (This may not be the most useful feature for a fifteen-year-old, but he or she will probably find it interesting.) You can also do a "check-by-phone," in case you've come down to the wire with a bill's due date and you don't want to incur finance charges or negatively affect your credit rating.

When I had my first real job in my late teens, I would get my check and carry it around in my pocket for days or even weeks. I would also wonder why I was always "a day late and a dollar short." I never quite equated the two things back then.

The advent of direct deposit allows employers to deposit your paycheck straight into your account. How cool is *that?* This saves you the trouble of having to go to the bank every week with your paycheck, stand in line, and wait to deposit it. Direct deposit also avoids the possibility of your check getting lost or stolen between the time you receive it and the time you deposit it. Electronic deposits save time and money and make your life more efficient and stress-free.

Remember the 10 percent you're paying yourself? You can have that money automatically taken out of your account and invested as you like. This feature is wonderful for people who simply do not have or cannot develop the discipline to invest on their own. A bank officer will be more than happy to explain to you exactly how to set up such an investment.

Most of us who grew up in the inner city or a low-income neighborhood tend to lump together all authority figures—police, judges, anyone who wears a uniform or sits behind a desk—as "the enemy." Whatever your feelings about those authority figures, they do not apply here. Your local bank officers are a completely different story.

If you have money to deposit, save, or invest, the banker is your best friend. Bankers actually *want* to have a personal relationship with you and tell you about all the services they offer. Remember that you are a customer, and a business can never have enough good customers. Even if you bounce checks, they'll still make plenty of money off you! Bank officers will take the time to explain the different options and features available for saving, investing, and even borrowing, when the time comes. Look at them as allies, providers of information—not as people out to get you.

Checking accounts are not for everyone. If you make less than $15,000 a year and live in a relatively large metropolitan area, you might be surprised to learn that you probably *shouldn't* have a checking account. Chances are you are living a "cash-and-carry" lifestyle. Remember that half of all American households are living paycheck to paycheck; they have no savings to buffer the inevitable times when that extra bit of cash is needed. This problem is magnified ten times over for people who make less than $15,000 a year (we're talking year 2002 dollars here).

With most traditional checking accounts, you must maintain a minimum balance, or you will be charged a monthly fee of $10 or more. If you write checks against money you do not currently have in the bank, you will incur additional charges. The banking industry refers to these as NSF, or "nonsufficient funds," charges. These figures can run as much as $25 or $30 *per bounced check!*

Will You Take a Check?

Say you deposit $500 and write checks totaling $700. That's an extra $200 the bank must pay to cover those checks. For each bounced check over the $500 amount, you will receive an NSF charge. If you have written three or four checks to total that $200, your NSF fees could run as high as $120! When you add up the monthly minimum fee along with potential bounced-check fees, you can see why a person earning under $15,000 a year doesn't really need a checking account. Fees could easily gobble up a sizable portion of that person's annual income.

Few things feel worse than depositing money against an existing negative balance. Take it from me. I've been there and it's depressing. As my friend Rodrick McGrew says, "It is a rush to the top of the bottom."

CHECK YOUR OPTIONS

For families who pay bills as cash becomes available, money orders and a responsible check-cashing operator offer a better approach for living within one's means. Managing your affairs in this way does not mean that you are acting irresponsibly with your family's affairs. It simply means that you handle your business in a different, less traditional manner. It is nothing to be ashamed of. You do not have to feel bad in front of your kids. If you are able to raise children on less than $15,000 a year in this country, America—and your kids—should be giving you a medal, rather than criticism or grief. My hat is off to you.

If you do run your finances in this manner, be sure to keep hard-copy records of each money order number, amount, and use. Of course, this means keeping a hand-crafted budget (as discussed earlier) and keeping a running tally of your total money spent in cash and money orders. There are ethical check-cashing operators out there. They might be the logical alternative for you.

Operation HOPE recently partnered with the Union Bank of California to acquire a combined 45 percent interest in Nix Check Cashing, the largest check casher in Los Angeles County. We teamed up with Nix at the indirect suggestion of my friend Judge Kevin Ross, an African American and the youngest judge in the state of California. Kevin, who is also quite practical, gives this advice: "When you are getting run out of town, get in front of the crowd and make like a parade!" In other words, turn a bad situation to your advantage. Richard Hartnack, the vice-chairman of Union Bank of California, agreed that the cooperative effort would be a successful way to help our community. "We decided that if you can't beat 'em, buy 'em!"

For as long as I can remember, traditional inner-city community leaders have been picketing against and complaining about check-cashing operators. The only thing that has changed is the number of check-cashing operations in the inner city. In South Central Los Angeles alone, check-cashing operations have multiplied like freedom in a former communist state. Yet all some so-called leaders do is complain or try to legislate them out of business without offering a viable alternative, such as encouraging banks in these communities, or educational outreach.

Then someone realized the potential. Nix Check Cashing alone has more than 600,000 registered, card-carrying customers. No one was forced at gunpoint to do business with Nix. Payday loans are a time-honored tradition in the inner city, but that doesn't mean they're actually *good* for people. Operation HOPE works with Nix to move people from the paycheck-cashing side of the ledger into the checking-account column. But it is a struggle. The reasons people continue to act in ways that prove contrary to their long-term interests are complicated, often involving the social and spiritual frameworks in which they were raised.

Ask around in your community or call Operation HOPE to find out who is the best check-cashing entity in your area. Again, my bottom line: if your family makes less than $15,000 a year, a checking account may not be for you. If your family makes more than that amount, the rest of this chapter is for you.

Will You Take a Check?

A checking account in America—a democracy founded in the tradition of economic prosperity and commercial trade—has come to symbolize more than the benefits it actually offers. These days, a traditional checking account "does" more than it was originally designed to do.

For the majority of Americans, the basic components of a standard adult lifestyle are a checking account in good standing, a driver's license or other form of valid government identification, a Social Security number, and a major credit card or bank card with a MasterCard or Visa endorsement. With these things, you are in pretty good shape. Without them, you'll waste a lot of time and energy in a mostly fruitless attempt to make merchants "comfortable" with doing business with you. But the beginning of everything, even your credit profile, is the checking account. Yes, your checking account is also a form of credit.

Earlier I noted what happens when you write checks against an NSF account. What I didn't mention was the added pain of being on a first-name basis with Telecheck and Telecredit. These central credit databases, used daily by banks, keep track of economic deadbeats. If you get in the habit of writing bad checks, you will first be fined the standard 10 percent to 50 percent in NSF fees. It only gets worse from there. With repeated misuse of your account, you will more or less be blackballed from the mainstream banking world. Sound harsh? Better to read about it in a book than experience it firsthand!

When I was ten, my friend Eddie's parents talked about having banking accounts, telephone bills, and rental agreements—in Eddie's name. These conversations made no sense to me. Eddie was only a little older than me. I kept wondering why I didn't have my own bank account or telephone. The reality was that my friend's parents had so messed up their personal credit history that they began *establishing new accounts in their child's name* (a sad and all too common occurrence, as I discussed earlier).

But I *know* that you will never end up in this unfortunate situation, so I will accentuate what happens when you do things right.

You work hard at your job, making deposits into your account and writing checks against this money with the understanding that some funds may have a three- to five-day hold if they are deposited from out-of-state companies. What's the bank doing all this time?

The bank isn't just sitting there collecting interest on your money (although it's certainly doing that, too). The bank is actually making constant and ongoing character assessments of you — based on your checking account. When a bank opens a checking account for you, they take on some measure of financial risk on your behalf. When you live up to your financial obligations and promises, the bank is inclined to have more faith in you. Why? Because every bank, company, and corporation in America is looking for more good customers. No one can ever have enough good customers, so the bank will be happiest if you become and remain one, too.

Believe me, the bank will take notice when you do the right thing. However, if after twelve or eighteen months of your being on your best financial behavior they don't recognize you as a great customer, then you're with the wrong bank. In that case, move your business to another institution that "gets it." In today's competitive environment, most banks will appreciate your business regardless of your race, creed, or color. Even banks are learning the basic truth that "green goes with everything."

The first sign that your bank has recognized your responsible checking history is something called overdraft protection, a sort of check-bouncing insurance for those in good standing. Let's suppose you have $1,000 in your bank account and $500 in overdraft protection. This means you can write checks for amounts up to a total of $1,500. Of course, you are expected to pay the overdraft amount promptly. Overdraft protection is not designed to be a term loan (a loan for a fixed amount of time) or long-term credit. It's simply there for convenience when emergencies arise — for those in good standing.

Will You Take a Check?

After receiving overdraft protection, don't be surprised if you then graduate to a personal line of credit or a credit card with a separate $1,000 to $5,000 limit. That's the way the game works.

PUTTING YOUR MONEY WHERE YOUR MOUTH IS

You probably know your children better than you know anyone else on the planet. If you think that your young teen is mature enough to handle the responsibility of a checking account, I recommend you take him or her down to the bank to open one. Impress upon your child the importance his or her signature now carries. A good name is something that no one—except you—can take away from you. Make it clear to your children that whenever they put their name on a check or other legally binding financial document, they are making a promise backed up not only by the money in their account but also by their good name.

I'm not just talking about how the folks over at Telecheck and Telecredit feel about your kids. I'm referring to how they feel about themselves. You want them to have the idea that a checking account is the financial equivalent of driving a car. They're going out into a world of strangers where they need to be responsible for both their fiscal and physical actions.

You might ask, "Why does my thirteen-year-old need a checking account? What bills is she paying?" Again, the answer is all about habits. I want your children to start developing good banking habits when they're young because that's the way they'll handle money as adults. Responsible financial habits are learned at home.

When you go to the bank to discuss a checking account for your child, prepare to be overwhelmed by all the options available. Banks offer a variety of checking accounts for people in different situations. The accounts vary in terms of monthly and per-check fees, minimum balance required, and overdraft protection. Be sure to ask the banker for recommendations for your child.

One last item you should consider when your child is getting his or her first checkbook: the design of the checks. This may seem like an insignificant issue, but it's actually very important. When I was a boy, you could get checks in any color and style you wanted, as long as they were green with no pictures on them. Then, in the '70s, they started to put designs of horses, sunsets, and palm trees on checks. Today you can get anything from Mickey Mouse to Mickey Mantle on your checks.

Although I try not to be a killjoy, I am 100 percent dead set against kids getting cute checks. Despite their being made of shreddable paper, checks are money. The more they look like toys or games, the less likely they are going to promote financial responsibility. Tell your son or daughter that, at least for the first year, their checks will be plain with no designs. After a full year of responsible behavior regarding their account, they can order any kind of checks they want (provided they pay for the new design, of course). But for the beginning, keep it simple — and keep it green.

It's only natural that your child is going to want to start writing checks for everything in sight. It's hard to control that initial exuberance. But there's nothing like going through all the money in your account and suddenly realizing that you're out of cash to teach a person that you can only spend what you've actually banked. That's yet one more reason why a checking account for your teenage child is an indispensable tool in the process of getting your kids right with money.

PART 4

The Financially Literate High School Student

My First Job (I Hate Taxes!)

*I don't get an allowance but when I need money to go to the mall or some-
thing, my dad will give me a contract which says that in order to get $10, I
have to pull the weeds or whatever. If I don't pull the weeds or whatever it
says on the contract, then I have to pay interest back on the money . . . like
two dollars a week.*

MARYBETH FINNEGAN, BANKING ON OUR FUTURE
PARTICIPANT, AGE TWELVE

For many of us, financial planning means trying not to have
too much month at the end of the money. In this chapter,
I'd like to explore with you some ways to teach your high school kids
about moving forward financially, especially when they have their
own small income.

THE RETURN OF THE LEDGER

We've already discussed the evil of vagueness in our financial lives.
Chances are that your kids are responsible for chores around the
house. Add to this list of chores the responsibility of writing down
their spending.

Better yet, find a way for them to feel that they *get* to do this instead of feeling that they've *got* to do this. You want to teach your

kids that having money is a privilege, no matter how much or how little they have. Money is a form of power, but it needs to be treated properly or it will just go somewhere else. Teach your kids that while most people are vague about their finances, that's not how it works in *your* household. You can even attach a reward to this new responsibility. For example, put a little bonus in their allowance if they write down their spending. If they don't write down their spending, then it's up to you to think of some appropriate loss that they must suffer as a result—in addition to the loss in financial knowledge they'll already suffer. The key is to be fair and proportionate in terms of both the rewards and the consequences, and then keep your word.

It's hard to be vague or confused about the whereabouts of money when the numbers are staring you in the face. The ledger is perhaps the single most powerful financial tool that I can offer you and your family, and that's why you should instill the practice of using it in your children from an early age.

Sometimes, of course, we all fall a couple of days behind. You can teach your kids to reconstruct their day. "Where did you go first? And then where did you go after that? And after that?" In so doing, they can pretty much figure out where they went—and therefore what they spent.

Don't let the kids keep the ledger in their room. Keep it in a common area, such as the kitchen, and make it your job to check it daily to make sure it's being updated. Although this may seem like nagging, it's every bit as important as keeping after them about brushing their teeth or doing their homework. Successful people know exactly what they earn, what they earned last year, what they expect to earn next year, what everything in their life costs, how much they save, what their investments are doing, and everything else to do with their finances. That's why they're so successful—they know what's going on with their money. Most wealthy self-made people knew what their dollars were up to. They got to a point where their money was working for them instead of the other way around.

My First Job (I Hate Taxes!)

I frequently meet people with six-figure salaries and only $163 in the bank. They have absolutely no idea of how much they have or how much they owe. They write checks as if they were playing roulette at a Las Vegas casino: maybe they'll clear, maybe they won't. Their credit reports look like battlefields. This is no way to live, and yet countless Americans—even high earners—do live this way.

A lot of people in this country think that because they make a lot of money, they're rich. They aren't rich, they simply spend as if they were. This way of life is all too easy to fall into. *Do not let your kids develop these bad habits.*

TAKING TAXES INTO ACCOUNT

The worst thing about getting your first job is receiving your first check. Instead of being the triumphant moment it's meant to be, seeing the digits that declare the grand total can sock you a blow. How can the number be so *low*? You did the math, multiplying the number of hours you worked by your hourly rate. However, the number on the check is woefully small in comparison. "We wuz robbed!" you declare.

Yes, you were robbed. Your pocket was picked by the greatest professional in the history of pickpocketing—Uncle Sam. Not only did he take a little for himself, but so did your friendly state government, and if you live in a big city like New York, the Big Apple took a bite, too. But it doesn't stop there. You might also see deductions for Social Security, FICA, medical insurance, and so on. Yes, it's terrible to see that not every dollar you've earned goes directly into your pocket. The first time your son or daughter experiences this rite of passage is the perfect time to have a little talk about taxes.

Everybody needs to know about taxes, because you are going to pay more in taxes than you will for anything else in your life. You will never pay as much for your home, your clothing, food, cars, or any other item in your budget. The fact is that it costs a lot of money to run a government, whether or not you agree with the way the government spends it. The following is a friendly introduction to the tax system that will help you answer questions your kids might have.

The funny thing about taxes (if anything about taxes can be considered funny) is that the whole system is supposed to be considered "voluntary." That's right. People are supposed to "volunteer" to pay their taxes! However, the way it works is that if you don't "volunteer" to pay your taxes, the government will "volunteer" you for a nice spell in jail!

The federal tax system is so complex that people who go to law school generally study that subject alone for an entire year—and they still barely scratch the surface. Attorneys who wish to practice tax law actually need to go *back* to school an additional year for an L.L.M. degree. The very complexity of the tax code guarantees full employment for attorneys, accountants, tax specialists, and, of course, the Internal Revenue Service. Multitudes of people make barrels of money simply because the tax code is so complicated.

Having said that, I think you'll understand when I tell you that this book is not the place for a long legal dissertation. However, the crux of the tax matter can be summed up: you owe 'em, and the government collects 'em.

WHY AVOID AND EVADE AREN'T SYNONYMS

Here's something important to remember: tax avoidance is good, while tax evasion is *bad*. So what's the difference?

Tax avoidance occurs when you become familiar with the parts of the tax code that apply to your situation, such as child-care credits, education credits, and IRAs (Individual Retirement Accounts), that allow you to protect, or "shelter," some income from the tax man. When you take advantage of these special programs, you are not doing anything illegal. You are legally *avoiding* taxes that you would otherwise owe. Much of the tax code is based on policy decisions, which means that the government has certain goals or desires that it wishes to see accomplished. In order to reach these goals, the government gives tax breaks to individuals, groups, and businesses so that those desires might become reality.

For example, the government wants children to be educated. Educated children have the best chance of becoming responsible adults. The government will actually reduce your tax bill if you spend for the education of your children. It's your job as a parent to find out what tax credits out there will help you save for your children's education.

There is no reason for you to pay $1 more in tax than you should. Anything you can do to reduce your tax bill — within legal means — I am completely in favor of. Every year at tax time, a number of publishers produce big fat volumes of information about taxes. The best known include Prentice-Hall and J. K. Lasser. You can find them in the bookstore or the reference section of your public library.

Here's another opportunity for a financial field trip. Spend one of your family financial summits at the public library and go over these tax books. What they lack in romance and plot they more than make up for in clear, easy-to-follow information about ways to reduce your tax bill. Your kids will probably find the information more interesting than you do. You might give them a bonus: for every $10 in tax savings they find, they will get $2 from you to keep. Everybody wins! (Except the government, but that's their problem.)

Finding methods of tax avoidance, however, is completely different from tax evasion. Tax evasion is wrong for a number of reasons. First of all, it's against the law. We don't want to train our kids to break the law. Second of all, everybody in this society has to pull his or her fair share. We don't want to teach our kids to be free riders, taking advantage of the hard work of other people.

There is a third reason to avoid tax evasion, and that is a spiritual reason. Whenever I see people cheating on their taxes, I know that deep down they are operating out of a spiritual void. They do not believe that a loving God will take care of them and meet their needs. Instead, they feel that they are all alone in the world, and so they have to chisel and cheat to get every penny they can get their hands on. I don't believe this is necessary. I do believe that a loving God will take care of you and your family's finances, if you let Him.

Although there are thousands of methods of tax evasion, the most common methods include not declaring all of your income and inflating your deductions. *Do not give into the temptation to do either of these, no matter how foolproof they may seem.* You cannot make enough money from such a scam to make up for your children's lack of respect. Kids who see their parents cheat—on each other, on their taxes, or even at Monopoly—lose respect for their parents, and eventually lose respect for themselves. In case you have forgotten this from your own childhood, children believe that they are destined to come out exactly the way their parents did. If they see that their parents are dishonest and unable to lead responsible lives, they will believe that they themselves are destined to be just as dishonest. This is not the message we want to send our kids. No amount of money that you could possibly make from running scams will offset the damage you do to your kids. Somehow kids always know. If you think termites can do a lot of damage, you ought to see what moral rot can do to children. For everyone's sake, play it straight. Pay what you owe, not a penny less—but not a penny more, either!

FLIPPING BURGERS FOR DENTURES

When your child gets her first job, she will be asked to fill out a W-4. On this form, she will be asked for her Social Security number and how many exemptions she is taking. Your child may be able to write "exempt" on the form and not have any withholdings.

If your child earns under a certain threshold of income (in 2001, it was $4,400) your child will owe *no taxes at all* (that's what "exempt" means). However, if your child is likely to earn above that threshold, she will have to pay taxes. That's the bad news. The good news is that this ushers in yet another opportunity to learn about financial planning. Believe it or not, your child is eligible to start her own retirement plan!

This may seem like a bizarre idea, especially to parents without retirement plans of their own. But any individual who earns above the income threshold in a given year is entitled to contribute—tax-free—to a retirement account. If you still think this concept is crazy, consider this: if she starts early enough and contributes just $50 a month on a regular basis, by the time she is fifty, your child will be a millionaire. The idea of becoming a millionaire simply by putting a dollar or two a day in the bank surely would have a certain amount of appeal to a teenager. Tell a teenager, "You can't have those expensive sunglasses," and you are likely to incite rebellion. But tell that same child, "If you don't buy the sunglasses, you can put that money in your retirement account and become a millionaire a little sooner," you might be surprised which way the child goes.

Ninety-five percent of the United States' population is either dead or dead broke by the time they reach sixty-five. Most people, especially the working class, look at Social Security as their sole retirement plan, a purpose it was never intended for. However, the vast number of Americans lacking an additional retirement plan has pushed Social Security into that role. The problem with relying solely on Social Security for retirement is that it doesn't pay very much. Although some people believe that Social Security is at risk of vanishing, it's more than likely here to stay. That doesn't mean it should act as a substitute for a bona fide retirement plan.

IRAs (Individual Retirement Accounts) are one of the most popular methods of planning for the golden years. What some people don't realize is that, despite their name, they also serve many other purposes. An IRA can act as a place to put aside money for that proverbial rainy day. Even if it never rains, it's nice to know there's a stash of cash waiting for you should you need it. IRAs also allow for certain penalty-free withdrawals prior to retirement. Education is one of them. An IRA can serve as a high-yield college fund as well as a retirement plan. (We'll discuss this further in the next chapter.)

You can establish an education IRA for your children while they are still young. This allows you to contribute money on a tax-free basis each year. The money is invested in a variety of ways, depending on your tolerance for risk. When your child is ready to attend college, the money can be withdrawn from the education IRA. Here's the best news: you do not pay any taxes on the money your investments have earned in that education IRA. Yes, it's true. Uncle Sam *wants* your child to go to college, and here's the proof!

If your child opens a retirement account, she'll be able to see that a small amount of money invested on a regular basis leads to great rewards. In order to succeed, people need to be shown that success is indeed attainable. Most inner-city teens believe that their only chance of becoming a millionaire is by becoming a recording star or a lottery pick in the NBA. The percentage of teenagers who will go on to become NBA players is so minuscule as to be laughable, but playing basketball is pretty much the only long-term financial planning that many inner-city teens engage in. And how many aspiring rappers and musicians get recording contracts?

We're here to change all that. No matter what they do to entertain themselves, teenagers need to spend time getting serious about their financial needs as well. It's hard to get a child to delay gratification if it appears that gratification will never come. But when you teach a child that an investment of only $50 a month can lead to millionaire status or the opportunity to attend college, being financially self-sufficient becomes an attainable goal. If you work through the math and show your child the cold hard facts, he will say, "Hey! I *can* do this! I can succeed financially on my own!"

Well-to-do children are fed this confidence along with their mother's milk. They just *know* they are destined for success. The difference in lower-income homes is that kids often expect to fail. They don't expect to make money in any field other than basketball or entertainment. We cannot blame our children for those expectations. Except for dealing drugs, these might be the only avenues to success that many inner-city kids have ever heard of—and they most likely come from us. But by showing children that a regular, small investment in a retirement fund can lead to wealth later on,

My First Job (I Hate Taxes!)

we are completely revising our children's expectations. The higher the expectations, the more likely they are to succeed.

So, friend, taxes can actually be a blessing in disguise. While the uninformed teen will view taxes as a nuisance, the educated teen can use knowledge to plan for a comfortable future. Uncle Sam taketh away, but on rare occasions Uncle Sam giveth back. It's our job to recognize such opportunities because he's not going to knock on our door and remind us. I can't promise that you're going to *love* to pay taxes, but at least I can make the amount you pay a little less painful.

A PERSONAL STORY

I would rather be chased by the mob than the federal government!

The last entity in the world you want on your back is the federal government or, in this case, the Internal Revenue Service. The IRS. And in California they have a sister that is almost as tough, and her name is the Franchise Tax Board.

Look, I could say a lot of nice-sounding things about why you should pay your local, state, and federal taxes: the benefit of a forced savings account called Social Security, and the money that goes from us to and for "public good," and so on. But frankly, the point here is even simpler. Find something else to screw around with! Pay your taxes.

I have personal experience here, unfortunately. I can remember two cases vividly, one personal and one with my business.

When I started out as an entrepreneur I did not have much money, and the little money I did have went into my new small business. I took no salary, and what little money the company made I religiously "re-invested" back into the business. I was spending almost all of my time on and in the business, so I really did not have many personal expenses (and no life, either, but that is another story). All I had was a car payment and my little apartment.

The company "advanced" funds to me to pay these minor bills. I thought nothing of it. This went on for years. I rationalized that "it was the least my stinking little business could do" to show me some appreciation. Well, I found out later that monies "advanced" by your employer but not repaid become income TO YOU! Wow.

I reasoned that for four or five years I had no income, and so I didn't have to file a tax return. WRONG. First of all, even if you have little to no income you are still supposed to file a return. Second, I was wrong on the first thing! I DID have income. It was all those dang advances. Well, all of this came crashing down on my naïve little head when I finally made a couple of bucks and decided it was time to file a return with Uncle Sam, and his sister the Franchise Tax Board. Ouch. Then came their question: where have you been all of my life? The penalties alone, from not filing and other associated sins, more than doubled the amount I owed.

Now, at this point I did the smart thing, and if you are in my position (I sincerely hope not!), I strongly encourage you to do the same. I came clean.

I told the IRS and the Franchise Tax Board the entire sordid story, accepted their looks of "You're not serious, are you?" and I cut a deal. And this is where my pastor, Dr. Cecil "Chip" Murray of the First A.M.E. Church, and his training came in handy. Dr. Murray always told me to "talk without being offensive, and to listen without being defensive." It worked like a charm. The agent I was assigned to was not a happy camper. She was picking for a fight, but I was not going to give her one. Never pull a psychological gun on someone when you know yours is empty!

She made me do a financial statement (which was good in a way, because I had never done one before! You know me, always trying to find the rainbow after the storm), and we figured out what I could afford. To the credit of the IRS, once we came to an agreement, they never once came back to me trying to renegotiate, which is more than I can say for a number of my friends and business associates over the years. I paid off the IRS and the Franchise Tax Board, and now I make sure that I file my returns, and pay my estimated taxes, every year!

My First Job (I Hate Taxes!)

The other lesson I learned involved my business, and the best of intentions. After the riots of 1992 I founded Operation HOPE with much of my own money. As the payroll for Operation HOPE grew, my company, Bryant Group, had to pay it because Operation HOPE had no money and no assets. This lasted for about eighteen months, until Operation HOPE could get on its own two feet, so to speak. No problem right? Wrong. Fast-forward to 1995.

One day, with no notice whatsoever, an IRS agent came knocking on my front door. They said that I owed more than $30,000 for "payroll taxes." I explained that Bryant Group was no longer an operating company, for one thing, and for another, I remembered paying payroll taxes for my employees of Bryant Group as I paid them every other week. Furthermore, I assumed that this was a non-issue because the company was not active, given my heavy involvement at that time with Operation HOPE. Wrong, wrong, wrong.

First of all, it appears that what I did was pay Operation HOPE employees with Bryant Group funds, but without taking any withholdings. But because Bryant Group paid them, my company was now liable for these taxes. Most painfully, I discovered, with payroll taxes, that if the company is not around anymore or cannot pay, guess who the IRS then comes looking for. That's right: the owner or principals of the company assume all tax liabilities of the corporation! This absolutely blew my mind, but I was not through learning lessons about the power of the government.

In typical John Bryant form, I decided I would deal with it and sort it out when I could schedule it, find the time, whatever. Wrong. The IRS notified me one day that they planned to lien my personal and business assets, and possibly even install an agent at my front door who would take all incoming receipts (a fancy way of saying "*my money!!!!!!!*"), from all sources, until the debt was satisfied. I had no idea that the IRS could do this, but believe me, I learned fast! I took out a loan and I paid off the $30,000 obligation, but quick.

Once I understood the government's power to collect taxes, you better believe the IRS became first on my payee list. I wanted the government out of my life, and I vowed never to be placed in a compromising situation again with the "feds."

Remember, my friend, the government finally got the infamous Al Capone not for murder and mayhem, but for tax evasion! That's right. Al Capone's reign of terror was brought to a screeching halt because he did not pay taxes on his ill-gotten gains. On the one hand, what he did was illegal and he should not have been doing it. And on the other hand—and this one still tickles me—if you do what you are not supposed to do and get away with it, the government still wants their cut!

In any case, the point here is simple and strong—PAY YOUR TAXES and encourage your kids to pay theirs. Keep those tax folks out of your living room . . . and your life!

CHAPTER 10

Credit Is a Privilege

I deposited $100 into my daughter's account and it was eaten up in over-draw fees. I called my daughter and asked if she had been keeping her bal-ance. Her response was that if she was using her debit card, the store should not have accepted her card for the purchase if she didn't have any money in her account. What I then shared with her was that if you run a whole bunch of purchases one after another, they won't catch up with the bank until the end of the day. Sooooo—I told her, it is critical for her to maintain a log of expenses and her balance so that she doesn't overdraw her account.

KAREN A. CLARK, MOTHER OF TWO TEENAGERS, BANKING ON OUR FUTURE PARTICIPANT

The most important asset your child can take into the world is a good name. The next most important is a good credit record.

As we discussed in an earlier chapter, every time we make a financial transaction, we are leaving footprints to be analyzed by various credit agencies. They are watching how we treat our money. For example, when we write checks, do we have enough money in the bank to cover those checks? When we take on long-term obligations like car payments, are we consistently on time? Do we ever skip payments? Everything we do involving credit is tracked by these companies' computers. You might say that it's not fair; it's like having Big Brother watch over your shoulder. However, these organizations are watching over us because we are living at least part of our lives with other people's money. Let me explain.

When we purchase an item via a method other than cash, we are actually walking out of the store without having paid for it. We're not shoplifting. It's just that instead of paying cash, we have left behind a promise to pay for that item. A check, therefore, is like an IOU. So is a credit card. With a check, we are making a promise that there is enough money in our bank account *right now* to cover that check. Otherwise, we are engaged in "hanging paper," otherwise known as bouncing or passing bad checks. Did you know that, in most states, deliberately passing bad checks is a felony? That's how seriously the government wants you to take your check-writing responsibility.

Similarly, when we pay by credit card, we are making a promise to eventually repay that money to the credit card company. The store does not wait until we pay Visa. The store collects from the credit card company within a few days. Next time you make a purchase, look for the little black box by the cash register. That terminal wires your credit card information to the store's bank. The bank then collects the money from the credit card issuer. Even though you left the store with a pile of CDs, the credit card company paid for them before you did.

Even though Visa wants to be repaid, they're betting that you won't pay on time. If you do, Visa doesn't make any money. (Unless your card is one of the few that still carry an annual fee, but *you* wouldn't have one of those archaic pieces of plastic!) Visa is really hoping that you do not pay off the balance in full, because that's when they really start to collect. My experience at Operation HOPE has taught me that some credit card companies are simply corporate loan sharks, ready to give you money now, but only if they can collect a whole lot more later on.

Credit Is a Privilege

If you pay your bills on time, whether you run a credit card balance or not, you develop what is called a good credit rating. Credit rating companies have put together what is called a "FICO score." A FICO score is a way of rating your credit history to determine just how likely you are to pay on any future obligations. The best FICO score a person can have is over 700, so people in that exalted group are called "700 club" members. Late bill payers and check bouncers are among those with FICO scores below 700 — sometimes way below 700.

Now don't scare your kids, but let them know that their credit history is being watched. Nobody's monitoring the way they spend *their* money. Rather, your kids are being watched for how they spend the money of *others*, namely credit card issuers and banks. Teach your kids that when they use a check or a credit card, they are paying with a promise as opposed to with cash. Since other people's money is involved in making those promises come true, at least in the short term, it's only natural that those institutions want to monitor just how well you keep your financial promises.

Credit is not a right. Nothing in the Constitution grants American citizens the right to bear credit cards. Teach your kids that credit is not a right but a *privilege*. If your kids take care of their credit responsibilities, they will enjoy excellent credit records. If they abuse those privileges, they will lose them.

In the old days, disobedient kids often faced the wrath of parents who were very imaginative when it came to punishments. Soap and belts were items to be feared (in your mouth and on your backside, respectively). We live in much more lenient times. It's hard to discipline your kids without their calling 911 and claiming child abuse. While this means kids can talk without blowing soap bubbles, it also means that most are not used to taking responsibility for their actions. Ringing up a new entertainment center on the Visa wouldn't appear to carry any major repercussions, but down the road it can mean the difference between being approved for a car loan or being laughed at. Don't let that happen to you, or your kids. Teach them that credit is a privilege that can be revoked at any time.

Once you've chiseled this idea into your children's brains, you can turn to the subject of interest. Introduce the idea that if they do not pay their credit card bill *in full* every month, they will owe interest. You might want to even walk them through what that interest rate might be on their credit cards. Teenagers tend to be the least responsible group when it comes to making financial commitments. As such, their credit cards carry the highest interest rates. Depending on what state you live in, you may well find that your kids' credit cards carry rates of as much as 22 percent! There's a word for this—usury, which means charging outrageous rates in interest.

MOM, MY VISA MELTED

If your teenage children do run up credit card debt and are carrying balances from month to month, you may want to introduce them to the idea of looking for credit cards that offer lower interest rates until they can pay off the balances. In the meantime, don't let 'em charge another penny!

I want to make a distinction between two different kinds of financial damage that we can do to ourselves. By carrying large loads of credit card debt, we are shooting ourselves in the pocketbook. Month after month, we are forcing ourselves to spend hard-earned money on items we have long since forgotten about. Even if we already have a huge credit card debt, many of us continue to charge away, thus locking ourselves more tightly into a never-ending downward spiral. Despite that damage, we never actually harm our credit rating.

The only time we harm our credit rating—the FICO score I mentioned earlier—is when we fail to make a monthly payment on time or when we carry a very high credit card balance relative to the credit limit. By missing a payment or by carrying a very high balance, we have indicated that we are not a good risk. If we want to borrow money again in the future, we will be paying higher rates than people who make their payments on time or carry a low balance.

I want you and your kids to understand the difference between these situations. If we owe a lot on our credit cards, that damages our financial position. If we don't make timely payments, that damages our credit rating and our future financial position.

Go online with your kids (if you don't know how, have them show you) and search for the words "credit card interest rates." Up on your screen will pop lists of banks across the country that have low-balance transfer rates for credit card debt. Write down the contact information for your new best friend. Your kids will be very excited to find out that they can lower the cost of their monthly debt payments if they switch to a credit card with a lower interest rate. However, they will still have to pay off the debt.

Here comes the hard part for you. They may cry. They may plead. They may promise to nominate you for Parent of the Year. No matter what they do, *do not pay off the debt for them*. The only way teenagers will learn that they are responsible for their spending is by facing the consequences of their actions. It may seem harsh to make teens spend most of their summer paying off credit card debt incurred a year or two earlier. But a teenager who endures this most dreadful experience is far less likely to get into trouble as an adult and rack up huge amounts of debt later on.

CREDIT WHERE CREDIT IS DUE

It's important for young people to establish good credit. Good credit means a history of borrowing and repaying money. You establish good credit by having a checking account, keeping it balanced, and not bouncing checks. You enhance it by getting a credit card and using it responsibly, ideally paying off the balance each month. When your child is old enough, he may even wish to take out a small bank loan—for his first car or a computer for college, for example—and pay it back within six months, just to further enhance his credit record. A good credit record established early will make an enormous difference when your child leaves home and rents his first apartment or shops for a new car.

Take your child to a used car dealer and find out the interest rate for teenagers with bad credit. Pick your kid's chin up off the floor, then take him to an established car dealer and ask to speak to the credit manager. Ask about rates for young people with good credit records. Both of those cars—the used car with the high interest rate and the new car with the low interest rate—will cost about the same. However, no kid wants to pay out of pocket to drive a crummy old vehicle when he could be driving something much nicer. I cannot think of a more graphic illustration of how to show your kids the value of a good credit record.

Sometimes mistakes creep into credit reports. Perhaps someone transposed two numbers on your son's report. Or your daughter has the same name as a woman with horrible credit. Thieves can get hold of Social Security numbers and "borrow" the entire credit profile of an individual. Although they are rare, such things do happen. Therefore, it's necessary to teach your kids how to check out and clean up their credit records.

The good news is it isn't hard. You can get a copy of your credit record for free or for a nominal amount from the credit record companies themselves, such as Trans Union, Experian, or Equifax. You can find them on the Internet. Alternatively, if your child has been turned down for credit and you suspect some sort of mistake, go with your child to an Operation HOPE office or an office of the Consumer Credit Counseling Service (CCCS). These nonprofit groups specialize in helping individuals regain solid credit. Either one can run a credit report and examine it with your child to determine where mistakes might have crept in. It does take a certain amount of persistence to get credit reporting companies to erase mistakes from their files; some companies specialize in helping individuals clean up their credit. (Before choosing one, make sure you do your homework on them. Call Operation HOPE for a list of referrals, or check with your Better Business Bureau.) If you are persistent, you can generally get a credit record cleaned up in a matter of months.

Credit Is a Privilege

Credit, like watching TV, is a privilege. And just like with watching TV, we can lose that privilege if our behavior does not meet certain standards. What's more, we need to maintain a good credit record or risk paying inflated interest rates—or, worse, having our credit history ruined for the future. Sometimes, through no fault of our own, our credit report gets dinged up and we have to make special efforts to repair it. It's all part of real life, and that's exactly what you're working so hard to prepare your kids for. I salute you for doing so!

WHY THERE'S NO PLACE LIKE HOME

In this section, I would like to explore with you and your teenage children the concept of secured versus unsecured debt. This is the key to knowing when to use a credit card and when to pay with cash.

Secured debt means that the lender feels secure because if you stop paying on that loan, there's a piece of property—usually a vehicle or home—they can reclaim. As long as the lender can hire a repo man to take your car, he sleeps easily at night. How you sleep is another matter.

Unsecured debt, by contrast, means any debt that is *not* backed up by a piece of property. If your teen goes out and buys groceries and puts down a Visa card, she has essentially made an unsecured loan. There is nothing for the lender to feel secure about other than your daughter's promise to pay the credit card bill when it comes in. If your daughter doesn't pay her bill and the food's already been eaten, the credit card issuer is just plain out of luck.

Most credit card borrowing is unsecured. If your son buys an electric guitar with his MasterCard, it's highly unlikely that MasterCard will try to repossess his Fender Stratocaster. (You may not want to tell him that. You may want to leave the impression that somebody's going to come and take that guitar right out of his hands.) But the bottom line is this: what exactly is MasterCard going to do with a used Stratocaster? Start a band? (I hope not.) They don't want the guitar back. They want their money. So an unsecured loan can also refer to anything for which the lender does not have a security *interest*.

Why would anyone want to lend money on an unsecured basis? This is a great question to sit down and discuss with your kids. Let's see what answers they come up with. (Send them to me. I can use a good laugh once in a while.) You and I both know that it all boils down to money. Lending money on an unsecured basis is an outstanding business to be in. You borrow money from a bank at 7 to 8 percent and lend it out to consumers at 20 percent. That means that for every $1,000 "in play," you're making $110, or 12 percent on your money!

Secured loans, on the other hand, generally have much lower rates of interest. If people had to pay 21 percent for a home loan, very few Americans would be homeowners. Generally, a home loan today runs between 7 and 9 percent. Car loans generally range between 8 and 10 percent, although you can often find "sales" on interest rates for new cars (as low as 0 to 0.9 percent). You might ask why a lender would take such a low percentage on a secured loan when they could turn around and make an unsecured loan for 18 percent to 22 percent. You might ask your kids why, too.

The answer is security. If you walk away and don't pay off your credit card, the bank is out of luck. They've got nothing to show for it. If, on the other hand, you stop making house payments, before you know it, everything you own is piled up on the sidewalk for all your neighbors to stare at. Forget to make your car payments and watch how fast the repo man makes an appearance. Lenders are willing to accept a lower interest rate on your loan in exchange for the security that comes from knowing that your property is available to be taken back if you stop making the payments.

Who Needs Security?

So why would anybody want to take out a secured loan? The answer's very simple: the bank takes our stuff away only if we consistently fail to pay for it. If we're late for one or two months, they're not going to throw us out of the house. As long as we keep making our payments, we will be fine.

You might want to ask your kids why they would want to buy a house when they can rent. If you rent, you can call the landlord whenever something goes wrong. He'll have to both fix it *and* pay for it. Miraculous! When it's your own home, you are responsible, no one else. If the roof goes, you have to pay for it. When property taxes come due, they come out of your pocket. Why would anyone want to *buy* a house?

Put this question to your kids and see what answers they come up with. Fortunately, you have this book in your hands, so I'll give you some answers to offer them if they don't come up with anything on their own.

There are a lot of great reasons to buy a house. First of all, there's pride of ownership. When you own your own home, you suddenly care a lot more about the neighborhood. You get angry when neighbors have brown lawns rotting away or dilapidated cars sitting up on blocks in their driveway. If a pothole in front of your house needs fixing, you are a lot more likely to call the city and get them over there to fix it. You just *care* more. Homeowners feel a lot more involved in their community than renters do. They are the stakeholders of the community. After all, if a neighborhood declines, a renter can just pick up and move somewhere else. A homeowner may have to watch the value of her house fall or even plummet.

Another reason for becoming a homeowner is the potential for investment. When your home goes up in value, which over time it almost assuredly will, you make a lot more money than you would on virtually any other kind of investment. Let's say that a home costs $100,000. In order to buy that home, with a secured loan, a typical down payment might be $10,000. Over a period of ten years, the home might double in value. (In the period from the early 1970s to the late 1990s, some areas of the country saw homes increase in price as much as *seven times over*.) It's now worth $200,000. Did your money double in value? No. It went up ten times — 1,000 percent. Remember that you only put down $10,000. If you sold your house, you would get back the $10,000 down payment, plus the $100,000 gain in price, plus a little bit more (the amount of monthly equity payments you made with your mortgage; more on that in a moment).

Right now, I just want your family to understand that you can "leverage" your money by investing in your own home. If your house is in a neighborhood that is increasing in value, you might be able to turn that $10,000 into $110,000—or more. If you take extra special care of your house, it may even rise in value more than your neighbors'.

You do not have to sell your house in order to take advantage of the gain in its value. You can get what is called a "home equity loan" or a "home equity line of credit." This means that a bank will lend you money on the difference between what your home is worth and what you paid for it. If you paid only half of what your $200,000 home is worth, you can get a certain amount of the remaining $100,000 as a loan.

Let's say that a bank will give you a $50,000 home equity loan or line of credit. You have several options with that money (the "equity"). You can take that money and start a business, or buy a small apartment building and be a landlord. (Imagine people writing rent checks to you! Wouldn't that be a refreshing change?) Or invest in the stock market. Or pay for higher education—either your kids' or your own.

However you spend the equity, make sure you spend it *wisely*. Don't spend it on a trip to Tierra del Fuego or Paris. Remember, this equity is a line of credit or a loan, both of which must be repaid. Eventually, you've got to pay back every dime. Most people just think of home equity as free money. Sometimes it even comes in the form of a charge card! That's probably not the best idea for those of us who have a hard time keeping our charge cards in our pockets. It's very easy to dribble away large amounts of home equity loans and lines of credit on impulse purchases and trips. The problem is that if you owe too much money on your house, you may not be able

Credit Is a Privilege

to make both the mortgage payment and the payment on the home equity loan or line of credit. That's when the sheriff comes and boots you out. So you want to be extremely careful about the way you use home equity loans and lines of credit.

Curses! Foiled Again!

In addition to these numerous home-owning benefits, there's yet one more I'd like to share with you. Home ownership is an outstanding way to foil the tax man.

Every time you make a mortgage payment, you are actually making two different kinds of payments on your house. One payment is the principal (the amount you actually owe on the loan). In the beginning of the loan period, this payment is a minuscule portion of the total. The greater part of your loan—about 80 percent—is interest. That's the bad news. The good news is that you can legally deduct this interest from your gross income when you do your taxes. In other words, interest payments that are part of your mortgage payment are tax deductible. This reduces your tax burden considerably.

Why is that? Because the government *wants* you to be a homeowner. When people own their own homes, neighborhoods are stable. People care more, as we discussed earlier. Homeowners make improvements on their property, so the companies who manufacture homes and home-building products have given your congresspeople a lot of money to make sure that those tax breaks for homeowners never go away.

These deductions make it possible for many people to own homes, even individuals who believe they can't afford it. At Operation HOPE, we've shown renters exactly what payments are necessary for them to own either the home they are currently renting or one much like it. They often discover that because of the tax break involved, they will not have to pay a penny more—and they also reap all the benefits of home ownership.

Plenty of government programs help low-income individuals and families make down payments, so the down payment is often not as big a sticking point as people think.

The bottom line is that a secured loan on a house makes possible the purchase of a home at a relatively low interest rate, which in turn allows you to enjoy all the benefits of home ownership that wealthy people enjoy. I'll let you in on a secret about wealthy people: the most common way for people to obtain wealth is by owning their own home, then buying more real estate with equity. Now you can get started on that same path to success.

A-House Hunting We Will Go

Let's say that your credit is ready and you have your down payment. Now it's time to start looking for a home.

You can find houses in the classified section of the newspaper, online, or with a realtor. If you choose to go with the latter, make sure you get firsthand recommendations. This is not the time to entrust your newly licensed brother-in-law with the largest purchase of your life. You need a trained professional who has access to all the houses in your area and who can negotiate on your behalf. Only go for the best when it comes to a real estate broker. You'll need an honest professional on your side. If your chosen abode is desirable, there will usually be multiple offers—many people will try to buy that same house the same day. The decision often depends on the quality of your real estate broker, how much she advises you to offer or even how she presents you and your family to the seller. Sellers tend to be emotional about their house and want to see it end up in the hands of someone who will cherish it as much as they did. An experienced real estate agent will paint your family as deserving of the beautiful home you are seeking to buy.

If you want to enjoy your house hunting experience, keep your eyes peeled for open houses. An open house is literally that: a home that is open to inspection by the public, usually on weekend afternoons. You and your exceptionally well-behaved kids are more than

Credit Is a Privilege

welcome to wander into any house in America that displays an open house sign. Inside, the real estate agent in charge of selling the property will give you a tour of the house, as well as printed information regarding costs, size, taxes, special features, and so on.

If you're serious about owning a home, go to open houses even if you're still several months away from making a purchase. You'll begin to get a sense of costs and availability, crucial information in home-buying negotiations. After a few visits to open houses, you'll be like an old veteran of the housing industry.

Open houses can help prepare you for the day you're ready to make your purchase. Attending an open house lets you imagine owning a home like the one you're visiting. It helps you develop dreams of moving beyond your current status as a renter and stepping up to being a full-fledged *owner*. You'll also determine what features you are looking for (new kitchen, extra bathroom) and which are not necessarily requirements but would be nice (pool, fireplace, hardwood floors).

It never hurts to visit open houses in affluent neighborhoods. No one will hassle you. Simply drive into the nicest neighborhood, park your car in front of any open house sign you see, and wander in. It's none of their business that you drove up from the 'hood! Walk right in and act as if you can afford that house, even if it costs a couple of million dollars. Pretend you're an up-and-coming R&B star, if you like (just refrain from singing). Not only will you have fun, but also you'll begin to ask yourself how you can afford such a home. Why shouldn't you live in the biggest house on the block?

An Offer They Can't Refuse

Let's say you've found something you like. Now it's time to make an offer. The standard way to make an offer on a house is to sit down with your real estate broker and fill out an offer sheet. In short, the form commits you to buying the house at a certain price; you detail your down payment and the amount of the loan you will take out.

A word about real estate brokers. The key thing to remember

about them is this: they work for the seller, not the buyer. The seller pays the broker a commission, and so the broker is likely to be more loyal to the seller than to you. A good real estate broker will balance responsibilities to both parties and give the buyer a lot of helpful advice, but keep in mind that the person who needs to be looking out for your best interests is you. Making an offer on a house is no small thing. Part of the process involves a deposit, which is generally 3 percent of the cost of the house. For example, if you have your eyes on a home going for $100,000, you will be expected to write a check for $3,000. You may be able to write a smaller check if you are using a government program to buy your home.

How much should you offer? It all depends on the laws of supply and demand. By the time you are ready to make an offer, you will have educated yourself as to what homes go for in your preferred neighborhood. You will have been to open houses, so you will have a sense of what comparable properties cost. Your broker will discuss how quickly things are selling. You'll also have eyeballed the "For Sale" signs in your neighborhood—just how long do they hang out there?

The bottom line is this: the more desirable a house and the hotter the real estate market, the more you'll have to pay. Your broker will be able to help you decide whether the offering price is fair.

If your offer is accepted, you now get a period of time in which to have an inspection of your house. Don't skimp on this practice, because this is your chance to find out if your future home is a diamond in the rough or a lump of nasty old coal. This is when you discover the quality of the "big three": the roof, the plumbing, and the electrical system. If work needs to be done on any of these three, the inspection can foretell a large number of repair bills, thus providing you with some negotiating room. Unless you pay a qualified inspector to do a thorough job, you may end up discovering that the *price* of the house is not the actual *cost* of the house.

What you pay the seller is only one element in what it really costs to move in. If you have to pay to redo the roof, you may want to back out of your commitment to buy the house—that's your legal right.

Discuss this option with your real estate broker. But above all else, get an inspection done during your inspection period.

You'll also need homeowner's insurance on the house. Without insurance, it's highly unlikely that a lender will loan you enough to buy your dream home. Obtaining insurance is purely a matter of routine. Your real estate broker or Operation HOPE can walk you through that process.

Generally, all of these events take place within a thirty- to sixty-day period from the time the offer is accepted until the moment that ownership of the house actually shifts. The last step in buying a house is called the "closing," the event when everything changes hands: the money goes to the seller, and the keys and title go to you. In some states, a closing requires an attorney. In others, the real estate broker or mortgage lender handles the proceedings. After you've dotted your i's and crossed your t's, the property becomes yours! You'll never forget the moment when you pick up your keys, open the front door, and stand inside your new home! That's what the American dream is all about. And now it's something that you and your kids can aspire to.

In the next chapter, we'll take a look at the financial situation of three individuals and see what kind of loans they might qualify for as they seek to make their American dreams come true. Once you and your family have absorbed the material in this chapter and visited a couple of open houses, you'll be well on your way to figuring out how much home you can afford.

CHAPTER 11

How to Get a Home Loan

The best policeman you can have is a homeowner, and, quoting my friend and mentor, the late Ronald H. Brown, "The best family value you can have is a job!"

JOHN BRYANT

When a bank considers you for a home loan, they weigh six factors: employment, income, credit history, down payment, savings, and debt. This chapter will introduce you to a game you can play at your next family financial summit.

NEIGHBORHOODS RINGED IN RED

Below, I describe three individuals who are seeking home loans. Have your kids pretend they are loan officers given the task of deciding which, if any, should receive a loan for a $100,000 house.

Our first candidate is Arthur. Arthur has been working in construction for the last three years. His income is $28,000, and his credit history is good. He can put $20,000 down on a house and has an additional $10,000 in savings, but he owes $16,000 on his credit cards. His outrageous debt dates back to before he got married—when he was a bit of a free spender, if you know what I mean. Since Arthur married, he and his wife have been working hard to pay down that debt, and they've done a good job of building up savings.

How to Get a Home Loan

Our second candidate is Beatrice. For the past five years, Beatrice has worked as the assistant manager at the local supermarket, where she worked her way up from a position at the checkout counter. She makes $34,000 a year. Her credit history is excellent, but she has had a hard time saving money. She has $4,500 in savings. The good news is that she has no debt at all. Her parents taught her that debt is the devil's tool, and Beatrice believed them.

Our third candidate is Charlie. For the past seven years, Charlie has worked at the telephone company as an installer. He makes $36,000 a year. He has $24,000 in savings, of which he can use $15,000 as a down payment. He owes $8,000 in credit card debt. Charlie's problem, however, is that his credit history is not very good. Charlie went through a period where he let his bills pile up and ignored threatening letters from creditors. As a result, his FICO score is about 450—rather low for a home loan.

There you have 'em. Ask your children to rank the candidates in terms of who is the most credit-worthy. Your kids can look at Arthur, Beatrice, and Charlie and decide to give loans to one, two, or all of them—or none of them.

If your kids seem stumped at first, you can prompt them by asking which factors are the most important. Is a steady employment history the most significant? What about credit history? How important is income level? What about the size of the down payment? Does the debt level scare you? There are no absolute right or wrong answers. Let me explain why.

Here's a quick history lesson. In the bad old days, even just a few years ago, the answer as to which of these three individuals would receive a home loan would be . . . *none of the above*. That's right. Neither Arthur nor Beatrice nor Charlie would have gotten a loan. All of them would have been rejected—not so much because of their finances, but because of the neighborhoods in which they wanted to buy. Until 1977, banks routinely practiced something they called *redlining*. They would literally draw red lines on a map around neighborhoods, usually ones with large populations of people of color, they considered unworthy of home loans. Nearly all the inner cities of America were redlined by banks for decades. Redlining made it extremely difficult—if not impossible—for individuals who lived in inner-city neighborhoods to own their own homes.

Why did the banks do this? Racism was certainly a factor, but they justified their decision to redline inner-city neighborhoods on financial grounds. Their argument was that people in these areas were incapable of taking care of their homes and so were undeserving of the bank's money. Although redlining was outlawed by Congress in 1977 with the creation of the Community Reinvestment Act, the practice unfortunately did not vanish overnight.

Redlining was extremely destructive to many inner-city neighborhoods and was one of the factors in creating the kind of blight that you see in some pockets of these neighborhoods. Your kids need to know that banks may well have redlined their current neighborhood for decades. In many ways, that practice of redlining contributed to the decline of inner-city neighborhoods. Owners care about their neighborhoods more than renters do. If you own, you're invested. You have put down a chunk of your hard-earned savings, and you're going to make sure that nothing happens to interfere with the housing values in your neighborhood. If renters don't like their neighborhood, they simply pack up and leave. If a community is not permitted to develop a cadre of homeowners, there is no way it can possibly keep up with nicer, home-owning communities. It's just an economic fact of life: if residents are not allowed to buy, the neighborhood declines because no one is financially committed to where they live.

Most people—especially middle-class individuals who have never been to the inner city—assume that inner-city neighborhoods resemble downtown Beirut. Guns go off, drug deals happen, the crew of *Cops* runs through the streets. That's why, in the wake of Los Angeles's 1992 civil unrest, I organized bus tours for bankers who had never even been to South Central. I brought them into the 'hood for the first time in their lives. As we drove through the leafy, tree-lined streets of orderly houses, I could see the amazement on their faces. "Why, it looks like Ozzie and Harriet live here!" they said. "Why aren't we lending here?"

Why, indeed? I didn't push the point. It's not wise to point out someone's ignorance when you're trying to do business with them. But ten short years later, those same banks arranged more than $100 million worth of home loan commitments in Los Angeles's inner city, thanks to Operation HOPE. Thankfully, when redlining was exposed as a racist and cruel process, Congress declared it illegal. Today, the process of redlining has been effectively obliterated from the banking system.

A QUICK SAT LESSON

Back to our home loan candidates. Let's look at each of them in a slightly different light. Let's say that each goes to the bank on his or her own (without the benefit of an organization like Operation HOPE) and applies for a home loan based on the information we already discussed. It is entirely possible that all three would be rejected. Each of them has a financial factor that would be distressing to a lender. Arthur has a good credit history and can make a sizable down payment, but look how much debt he owes. He might have a hard time making a mortgage payment. What about Beatrice? Her credit history is excellent and she has no debt, but a bank might look askance at her low savings. With only $4,500 in savings, she can barely afford a conventional down payment. And then there's our friend Charlie. He earns the most of all three and has been with the same employer the longest. He can even put down a sizable down payment. He does have some credit card debt, but not nearly as much as Arthur. His problem: his credit history. It's too spotty. There are too many missed payments. His FICO score is just too low. Point out to your kids that each of these three individuals would be deemed marginal by the traditional way that banks score potential homeowners.

I want to introduce you to what your high school kids would call an "SAT word paradigm." The word "paradigm" comes from ancient Greek and means "way of looking at the world." A "paradigm shift" occurs when everybody in a society starts looking at things in a brand-new way. America has gone through three such "paradigm shifts," or major changes in thinking, and is on the verge of a fourth. The first paradigm shift in America's social fabric came with its liberation from Great Britain under the leadership of George Washington. The second occurred with America's liberation from the institution of slavery under Abraham Lincoln. The third paradigm shift came with America's liberation of its own consciousness under the tutelage of Dr. Martin Luther King, Jr. The civil rights movement brought white America to the realization that it was unconscionable to treat blacks and other minorities as second-class citizens. Thus began the era of voting rights, employment rights, housing rights, and all the other rights that today we often take for granted.

The focus of my work is the fourth paradigm: the achievement of economic justice in America by extending the benefits of the free enterprise system to the economically disenfranchised. I have dedicated my life to helping individuals who live outside America's economic system get in. I do this through my organization, Operation HOPE, and our work to turn renters into homeowners—and therefore stakeholders in their communities.

We're no longer talking about civil rights. We're talking about silver rights.

I coined the term the "fourth paradigm" to describe this coming change in American consciousness. The fourth paradigm builds upon the success of its three predecessors in American thought. Its foundation rests on the fact that in today's world, economic empowerment is the only way to stem poverty in our inner cities, and thus keep those inner cities from exploding into tragedy yet again. This fourth paradigm includes a shift away from dependence on government largesse and the bloated poverty bureaucracy it has spawned.

What does this mean for you and your kids? It means that you are entitled to the same economic rights as individuals who live in upper-middle-class and wealthy communities. Operation HOPE has educated banks so now they understand that inner cities are full of individuals just like you who *can* and *will* own their own homes. It's your job to educate yourself and your kids about the economic possibilities that await you, from college education to home ownership—all the subjects we talk about in this book.

Prior to Operation HOPE, it is likely that banks would have rejected all three of our home loan candidates. Either their financial shortcomings would have dragged them down, or redlining policies would have excluded them. Today, Arthur, Beatrice, and Charlie could get home loans because of organizations like Operation HOPE that work to clean up credit history, find loan programs that offer low down payments, and otherwise make home ownership available to people who live in previously redlined neighborhoods. If you can fog a mirror, you can own your own home. That's the purpose of Operation HOPE.

When you go over this exercise with your kids, make sure they understand how the bank's answers to our three home loan candidates have evolved over the past few decades. Back when redlining was a way of life, the answers were no, no, no. In the days following the banning of redlining, the answers for Arthur, Beatrice, and Charlie changed to probably not, probably not, and probably not. Today, in the era of the fourth paradigm, the answer is, increasingly, yes, yes, YES! By exposing your kids to this material, you will not only teach them a little-known fact of the banking industry, but also show them that they are potential homeowners in their own right.

CHAPTER 12

How Your Kids Can Afford College

Your kids can afford college. Just show them the way to start saving when they are young.

R. C. METZ, MOTHER OF TWO CHILDREN IN COLLEGE

Many of our fathers and grandfathers supported their families with nothing more than a high school education. That time in American history is over. A young person without a college degree has virtually no chance of competing in the job market. Parents in lower-income families are painfully aware of this. They bemoan the limitations that they perceive for their children.

Let the sun shine in! This chapter is full of ways for your children to attend college. A university degree can be a reality, not just a dream.

Much of the information in this chapter is drawn from the website College Is Possible (*www.collegeispossible.org*). Make that website your first stop when you are looking for information about funding college costs.

THE DREAM IS POSSIBLE

Neither private colleges nor state universities expect lower-income parents to fund their children's entire college education. Many of the parents we meet at Operation HOPE are under the false impression that a college education requires tens of thousands of dollars. Nothing could be further from the truth.

America has a great willingness to educate those with the desire and aptitude but not necessarily the resources. If anything, the fact that your children have thrived academically in a less-than-ideal high school setting will actually work in their favor. Colleges appreciate the struggles of lower-income families. If your children have worked hard academically to demonstrate that they are indeed motivated, the resources can be found. Let's see how to locate them.

Your children may be eligible for one of three different types of financial aid: grants and scholarships, loans, and work-study. Grants and scholarships do not need to be repaid, either by you or by your children. Imagine that! Loans, on the other hand, *do* need to be repaid. However, unlike other loans that we have discussed, educational loans carry much lower interest rates, and your children will not have to begin repaying them until after they have graduated from college and are in the workforce. In work-study programs, students receive aid in exchange for working on the college campus.

Much of student financial aid comes from the federal government. The rest comes from state governments, colleges and universities themselves, and other private sources. You may want to ask your employer whether it offers a scholarship program for children of employees.

Most aid is based on family income, and some scholarships, grants, and loans are available based on merit. You want to look for both kinds of aid.

When your child applies to college, you will be required to fill out a form listing your income and other financial information. The contribution that is expected from you varies with your income level, the number of children in your family, the number of parents, and the number of other family members attending college and university. While you will be expected to contribute something, it may be nowhere near the lion's share of the tuition bill.

Major federal programs benefit lower-income students and their families. The Pell Grant program provides more than $7 billion annually for nearly 4 million students at 6,000 colleges and universities. The Supplemental Education Opportunity Grant program, as well as state programs, also aids lower-income students.

The federal government may also loan you money for college. These programs, including the Federal Family Education Loan Program and the William D. Ford Direct Student Loan Program, put more than $33 *billion* into the hands of college and university students every year. In addition, the Perkins Loan Program provides low-interest loans to postgraduate students who demonstrate financial need.

All these years, Uncle Sam has been taking money out of your pocket. Now that your children are ready to attend college, he's finally ready to stuff some dollar bills back in. My advice: let him!

Uncle Sam also provides certain tax benefits to parents of college students. The Hope Scholarship Tax Credit allows parents to deduct up to $1,500 per student per year. Similarly, Lifetime Learning gives you additional credit for money spent on college. You can also take money out of an IRA—with no penalty—in order to pay for education.

The federal government recently introduced something called the Section 529 College Savings Plan. This tax law, effective January 1, 2002, allows you to save money for college in a tax-deferred plan. With a Section 529 Plan, you can pay for tuition, room, board, fees, books, and supplies for your college-age child. Make it a point to start a Section 529 Plan as soon as possible, even if it means putting in only $25 a month. Saving, as you've already learned, is addictive. Once you start putting a little bit of money away, you'll feel the urge increasing to sock away more and more. Throw everything you can into savings plans for your retirement and for your children's education.

Wealthy people enjoy access to the finest investment geniuses in the country. The wealthy often turn over their money to top Wall

Street–type firms, who decide where to invest it. Those firms employ individuals called "money managers" whose job is to review every possible stock and investment, then choose the best of these for their clients.

When you get your own Section 529 Plan, you suddenly have access to that same level of top professional investment managers. Your money will be working just as hard as the investments of wealthy people. Section 529 Plans can pay for expenses at any accredited college, university, trade school, or graduate school in the United States. And, yes, a grandparent can open a Section 529 Plan for a grandchild. So be sure to show this chapter to your parents!

FREE MONEY (FOR COLLEGE)!

Another source of important information is a website called Fastweb (*www.fastweb.com*). If you don't own a computer, I recommend that you go with your child to the local library to view this site. Fastweb asks for your name, address, ethnic or racial identification, and other information in order to match you with more than $1 billion in scholarships—money that you do not need to pay back. The few minutes it takes to fill out these Internet forms might yield more money than you could possibly hope to earn in a year.

Fastweb is a for-profit site, which means that unless you opt out of some of the preferences, your e-mail box will be bombarded with spam (not the canned meat product, but junk e-mail). Simply check "no" for each option and see whether Fastweb's scholarship database can provide you with any leads on free money. If Fastweb seems helpful, you might want to change your preferences to receive notifications.

Unfortunately, you'll have to be wary on your quest for scholarship money. Many scholarship scams take advantage of the desperation that many parents and students feel as they seek to fund a college education. Follow this general rule: if you're asked to put up money, walk the other way. If you have to include a fee of even $5 in order to win a scholarship, it's probably a rip-off. The same is true if you are "awarded" a loan that requires an advance fee, or a scholarship that requires a "disbursement" or "redemption" fee.

Also be on the lookout for the "guaranteed scholarship search service." Any time you have to pay money for the guarantee that your child will win a scholarship, you can be certain it's a scam. If you get a letter advertising a free financial aid seminar, the seminar might include some good information, but chances are they are going to hit you up for expensive financial aid consulting services that you don't need. (Read more about common scholarship scams at *www.finaid.org*.)

A family financial summit would be a great time to research college scholarship and loan possibilities. Have your child search the web with such keywords as "college tuition," "scholarships," and "financial aid." The web is a rich source of information, and you might be amazed at what your child finds in only a matter of minutes.

This chapter is brief because I just want to give you some examples of what's out there and let you know that the money—and the information on how to get it—is available for you and your children. Your local library or bookstore carries books with information on colleges and scholarship opportunities. Never think of a college education for your children as an unattainable luxury. In today's America, it is the ultimate necessity. Your children cannot afford to be without a college education. The money and the information are out there. In short, your children are going to college.

CHAPTER 13

We Don't Live Forever

Though I walk through the valley of the shadow of death, I shall fear no evil,
for Thou art with me.

PSALM 23

No one wants to think about dying, and yet it's a part of life. A minister I know says that "death is the tax we pay for loving people." While you or I could win a million dollars in the lottery (although that's not the kind of financial planning I advise banking on), we cannot win a million hours. No one will live forever. In this chapter, we're going to tackle some of the life-and-death issues that most of us—heck, all of us—would like never to think about.

Many of us try hard never to contemplate our own mortality. I don't believe in dwelling on such matters, but I do believe in—and heartily recommend—making adequate preparations. I'd like to discuss with you two aspects of estate planning, which is what lawyers call making plans for if we die or become incapacitated. The first is the matter of your will. The second is what should happen to you in the event that you are unable to make your own health care decisions, due to accident or declining health. You may want to keep your will a private matter. Children don't need to know what's in their parents' will. However, health care decisions *absolutely* must be discussed with your older children. Let's first look at the question of the will.

Banking on Our Future

You may be saying, "John Bryant, what are you smoking? Why do I need a will? Do I look like some kind of rich person?" Yes, you do! You are rich with the love of your family. Let's clear away a common misconception: *wills aren't just for rich folk.* I don't care how much or how little you've got. You need a will. Period.

All of us have been at the mercy of a "system" at some point in our lives—welfare, Social Security, or health care. Perhaps you have shameful memories of the way your parents were treated by some rude, crude government clerk. Perhaps you've been through that mill yourself. If you don't have a will, guess who's going to be in charge of your financial life again. The government! It'll be a case of *They're Baaack!* And they're going to decide what will happen to you, your money, your home—even your kids.

That's right, your kids. If you don't have a will, the government will step in to decide who raises your children. They might choose someone you really don't want. Your children might be placed in a situation that you would consider inappropriate or just plain wrong. Do you really want the government taking its own sweet time deciding who should be raising your children in the event that you are no longer around to do so? Doubtful. But unless you specify a guardian in your will, the uncaring, uninterested, unloving local government will make that decision for you. Is that what you want? You'd better say no.

Wills have two main purposes. The first is to instruct the world exactly how you want to divide your assets—your home (if you own it), your car, your bank balance, your retirement or pension money, and all of your personal items such as clothing, household goods, and even your *pets* (Fluffy isn't immune). You don't want the government dividing up your stuff. They don't care about you. It'll be the old welfare/Social Security/health care nightmare all over again. You didn't work hard all your life to end up in the "care" of the government. And you certainly don't want relatives fighting over your stuff, rushing from your funeral to some lawyer's office to make claims on your home, car, photo albums, and everything else you've left behind.

Don't be foolish enough to think, "Not *my* family." Nobody fights like families. So don't put your family into a position where they *have* to fight.

The second purpose of a will is to indicate guardianship for your children. In a will, you specify not only who gets to raise your kids, but also how they should be raised. If you want them to visit their grandparents in a distant city twice a year, you can specify that in your will. If you want them to attend a certain school, such as a private religious school, you can specify that, too. You have rights . . . but only if you outline them specifically in a will.

In a will, you get to name an *executor*. As a lawyer friend of mine says, this person makes sure that "your wishes will be carried out once you're carried off so your family doesn't get carried away." The executor should be someone you trust completely. He or she will supervise the details of the will and see to it that people get exactly what you want them to have. If you choose a guardian for your children, the executor ensures that your wishes regarding their care are followed. Your executor may be in charge of the money you leave to your kids and can make certain that it's spent the way you intended: on education, travel to distant relatives, or whatever you specify. So choose your executor carefully.

You'll need either a lawyer or a legal clinic to draft the will. Drafting shouldn't be expensive because most likely you're not going to need a lot of fancy additions. Ask a few different lawyers how much they charge to draft a simple will. Contact law schools in your vicinity (check the Yellow Pages for listings); many run legal clinics offering free or low-cost services to low-income individuals. If not, they might be able to make other recommendations, including legal aid organizations such as public counsel.

One function of a well-drafted will is to avoid *probate*. Probate is a long, slow process by which the court makes sure that your will is legitimate. When a will is probated, it can take up to a year before people can get what you've left to them. Yes, even spouses are prohibited from receiving the deceased's money until the probate process is complete. Probate is something to avoid, and a good lawyer will show you how. Don't be afraid to ask your lawyer all the questions you can think of. Your lawyer's job is to answer your questions to the fullest extent possible. If you think he or she isn't being responsive, get another lawyer.

IN SICKNESS AND IN HEALTH

Let's move to the subject of your health care. None of us wants to think about it, but life is dangerous and sometimes cruel. A drunk driver coming down the street, a sudden illness that worsens—bad things do befall good people. We need to concentrate on what will happen if you are unable to make health care decisions for yourself.

You have two options. One is to be ostrich-like, stick your head in the sand, and say, "It'll never happen to me." Let me illustrate why this is *not* a great choice. Let's say something *does* happen to you. You're suddenly incapacitated and unable to make decisions for yourself. You can't even speak. What will the doctors do? *Whatever they feel like*. If they want to resuscitate you, they will. If they want to cut off your life support, they will. Your family won't know what you want and may even have contradictory opinions about what's best for you. Perhaps you have strong religious beliefs about your treatment. Who's going to know what those beliefs are? More important, how will that person have the authority to command the doctors to do what *you* want?

The answer is that right now, while you're healthy, you need to make those painful decisions and create a document that indicates exactly what your wishes are. The name of this document varies from state to state. In California, it's called an "Advance Directive for Health Care." In New York State, it's called a "Health Care Proxy." The document is very simple, and in many states you don't need a lawyer to create it. Chances are your kids can pull one off the Internet for you. Since each state has a different method of organizing state government, the easiest way to find the form and information about it is to use an online search engine like *www.google.com* or *www.altavista.com* and type in "Health Care Proxy" and the name of the state in which you live.

In the event that you can't make your own decisions about your health care, due to physical or mental incapacitation, this document goes into effect. It specifies:

1 Your *agent*—that is, the person you've chosen to make your health care decisions. You also choose backups in case your first choice is unable or unwilling.

2 What you want and don't want. Do you want to be resuscitated no matter what? If there's virtually no chance of your survival, at what point do you want to cease life-support measures? Do you want nutrition and hydration (food and water)? (You'd be surprised—hospitals often fail to provide patients with food and water! Many sick people actually die of malnutrition and thirst; make sure that doesn't happen to you.) Do you want to be an organ and/or tissue donor?

Here's the best part about these documents: *doctors are legally bound to follow them!* Whoever fills out a health care proxy retains power—not the doctors, and not a gaggle of relatives who show up at the hospital, each certain they know your heart's desires. Fill out one of these forms and give copies to your doctor (if you have one), your agent (the decision-maker), and your spouse or older children. Keep in mind that you can change the document any time and as often as you like. You may want to discuss the contents of the document with your religious leader, so that you are adhering to the tenets of your faith.

This document is something to discuss with your *older* children at a family financial summit. If they're high school age, they are probably mature enough to handle the thought of something bad happening to you. You might even choose one of your children as your agent or as a backup. Perhaps they will feel safer knowing there is someone to turn to if anything happens to you. They will be far more likely to take responsibility for such important matters in their own adult lives because they'll have your example to follow.

Banking on Our Future

Below is an example of the Health Care Proxy for New York State residents, to give you a sense of what the document looks like. Health care directives vary from state to state, so be sure to get the document for the state in which you live.

HEALTH CARE PROXY

(1) I, _____
hereby appoint _____
as my health care agent to make any and all health care decisions for me, except to the extent that I state otherwise. This proxy shall take effect when and if I become unable to make my own health care decisions.

(2) Optional instructions: I direct my agent to make health care decisions in accord with my wishes and limitations as stated below, or as he or she otherwise knows. (Attach additional pages if necessary.)

_____

_____

(Unless your agent knows your wishes about artificial nutrition and hydration [feeding tubes], your agent will not be allowed to make decisions about artificial nutrition and hydration. See instructions for samples of language you could use.)

(3) Name of substitute or fill-in agent if the person I appoint above is unable, unwilling, or unavailable to act as my health care agent.

_____

_____

(4) Unless I revoke it, this proxy shall remain in effect indefinitely, or until the date or conditions stated below. This proxy shall expire (specific date or conditions, if desired):

_____

(5) Signature _____

Address _____

Date _____

Statement by Witnesses (must be 18 or older):

I declare that the person who signed this document is personally known to me and appears to be of sound mind and acting of his or her own free will. He or she signed (or asked another to sign for him or her) this document in my presence.

Witness 1 _____

Address _____

Telephone number _____

Witness 2 _____

Address _____

Telephone number _____

That's it. Get yourself a will and a health care directive. Put them in a file marked "Just In Case," and keep the file where it can be found. Then forget about both of these documents, and go out and enjoy your life.

PART 5

Financial Fitness for Young Adults

CHAPTER 14

Investments:
You—Yes, You—
Can Get Rich...Slowly!

I can't imagine a better way to become a financially savvy adult than to be aware of finance as a child. I've had my own savings account since the age of five and, as an adult, I am now a proud homeowner. It was extremely important for me to acquire a sense of financial literacy as a child.

JENNIFER HUSTON, FIRST-GRADE TEACHER

We all know the expression that "money goes to money." In this chapter, I'd like to explain how some of that money can start going to you.

Here's a fun way to introduce your high school kids to stocks, bonds, and other investments. Let's say that your son wants to start a business selling T-shirts at rock concerts. He's going to need a certain amount of money to get started. Have him list his expenses: the cost of making the T-shirts, hiring people to sell them, advertising, and so on. Ask your son to come up with a figure for each of these expenses.

Let's say that advertising will cost $1,000. Your child has a few options for obtaining that money. First, he can borrow the money from a friend, a relative, or the bank—all options that require the payment of interest. If he pays 10 percent interest, he will have to pay back $1,100 ($1,000 principal and $100 interest). Now the cost of interest needs to get factored into the sale price of the T-shirts. You might want to point out that once your son has borrowed the $1,000 and repaid it with interest, he may not have enough money left to keep the business going. There's another way to finance a business, and that is by issuing stock. Let's take a look at how that works, so you can share this information with your kids.

When you issue stock in a company, you are basically selling pieces of that company to different investors. Let's say that your son has eight friends who are each willing to put in $100, for a total initial investment of $800. That means your son only has to come up with $200. Since each friend has contributed $100, each would be entitled to 10 percent of the company; your son keeps the last 20 percent. Now your son has the necessary money to start making and selling T-shirts. He does not need to repay that $1,000 because it is "invested" in the company. In other words, the money is not a loan. If your son "loses his shirts" and doesn't make a dime, the investors are simply out of luck. An investment means taking risks. It's as simple as that.

Of course, no one goes into investing to lose, so let's go with a happier scenario. Let's say that everybody adores your son's T-shirts. As a result, he is able to sell out the first run. Instead of having to repay the loan, as in the first example, he can plow all the profits back into the company, make more T-shirts, and sell them. After a period of six months, your son might sell $10,000 worth of T-shirts. At that point, what is the value of those eight initial investments of $100? What are they worth now?

That's a much harder question than it seems because it depends on a lot of factors. Does your son want to continue running the business or perhaps sell it to someone else? Does he want to add a second item to sell, such as baseball caps? Chances are, if the business is successful, the value of each of the shares of the company will increase, perhaps even substantially. Let's take a look at the numbers.

Our initial investors each put in $100, which bought them 10 percent of the company. In other words, if there were ten shares at first, eight of them belonged to the eight friends and two of them belonged to your son. Now, since the value of the business has increased, the friends might be able to sell their shares for $500. As the business gets stronger, the value of the shares will increase.

This small-business example illustrates what happens on Wall Street every day. Individuals own pieces of such successful businesses as Microsoft, Ford Motor Company, Coca-Cola—virtually any name you can think of. Those pieces, called "shares," are part of an enormous system that works on the same principle as your son's T-shirt company. Look at Microsoft on any given day and decide how it's doing. Are sales up or down? Are the new products good? Do people want to buy them? All of these factors determine how much anyone is willing to pay for a piece of a corporation. When you hear the stock market report that Ford was up one, that means that the cost of a single share of Ford stock went up $1 compared to the price at which it sold yesterday. If Microsoft went down $.50, it means that you can buy a share of Microsoft for $.50 less than it cost yesterday. Those are the basics of stock prices.

You can make the stock market a game with your kids. Go to *my.yahoo.com* and set up a personal page on which you can choose to watch a number of stocks. Have your kids choose a few stocks that interest them. Every week or even every day, they can check and see how the prices are doing. Make it a competition and they'll soon start to see it as fun.

THE FEELING'S MUTUAL

No one has the time or enough interest to examine the fortunes of every single corporation out there. Most of us are too busy doing our jobs and raising our families to spend endless hours staring at computer screens, scrutinizing stock market TV shows, and reading investment publications. As we discussed earlier, some people invest their money with money managers, who are specially trained to pick stocks that, at least in theory, have the best chance of going up. Money managers do all the footwork you would do if you had the time. They read about stocks that interest them, and buy and sell in order to maximize their clients' investments.

Money managers run what are called "mutual funds." Put simply, a mutual fund is a pool of money—sometimes in the tens of millions of dollars—that one person controls. That person invests the pool of money on behalf of all the individual investors, often people just like you. There are literally thousands of mutual funds to choose from. If you are very aggressive, enjoy risk, and have time to let your money grow, you can choose aggressive growth–type funds. For older investors who are more interested in a fixed income, some funds specialize in stocks that pay secure dividends.

There are mutual funds for every taste. One of the best places for specific information on mutual funds is Morningstar (*www.morningstar.com*), where the professionals learn how funds are doing. You and your kids ought to pay a visit to the website and get some extra education yourselves.

I know what you're thinking: "John, I make $25,000 a year and you want me to invest in Wall Street?" Yes, friend, I do! You don't need millions of dollars to start an investment portfolio. Perhaps you'd like to open one up with your children. For just $50 a month, you can start a mutual fund investment with a number of major companies, such as American Century (*www.americancentury.com*), one of the country's top-rated sellers of mutual funds. They are very interested in helping Americans of all economic levels become involved in investing. While some companies require a minimum investment of $2,000 or more, American Century has no minimum—as long as you are willing to commit to investing $50 a month. You can even arrange to have this amount automatically deducted from your bank account each month.

Investments: Yes, You *Can* Get Rich

Visit their website to see the sort of mutual funds available. After you've signed up, make periodic visits to the site to see how well your fund is doing. You'll find it exciting to watch that money grow.

HOME SWEET HOME

People often think that working-class families are incapable of saving money. That's just not true! At Operation HOPE, we frequently work with single, working-class parents and married couples who have managed to accumulate tidy sums of cash. One couple, a schoolteacher and a butcher, brought in a combined income of $50,000 a year. They managed to save nearly $60,000, which they kept, in cash, in a safe at the butcher shop. He simply didn't trust banks. I'll never forget the day they brought in all that cold cash — and that was *really* cold cash!

People who are able to save such amounts of money should consider investing in real estate. There are enormous financial and tax benefits for individuals who can make a down payment on a two-family home or a small apartment building. Buying real estate is not beyond your means. If you can develop a habit of saving, before you know it, you can be a landlord who *receives* checks every month instead of *writing* them.

When you buy a duplex or a two-family home, you live in one unit and rent out the other. You'll be able to write off depreciation, interest, and just about any improvements that you make on that combination home/investment. ("Depreciation" is a form of legal accounting magic that allows you to reduce your taxes if you own rental property.) If you've got cash hidden under the mattress or in a meat freezer, now may be time to take it out and plunk it down on a two-family home.

Once you own your own home and/or rental property for a few years, if the value goes up, you can take out some of that money in the form of an equity loan and buy another property. Before you know it, you can be a mini real estate mogul. Wealthy people become wealthier because they put money into assets that grow—stocks, bonds, and real estate. Many wealthy people I know started off with limited educational opportunities and little family wealth. Most are self-made individuals who began with the same slender resources that you might be working with. There are no limits to what you and your children can do when you learn about investment opportunities.

CHAPTER 15

Welcome to Wall Street!

Teaching students financial responsibility when they're young will ensure that they have the resources for financial stability when they are adults. I remember when I was a child, my uncle would have my cousins reading the business section of the newspaper and playing the stock market. They originally used play money but graduated to small amounts of real money as their Wall Street savvy increased. Today, they have very secure financial portfolios.

MARY ELLEN FOX, FOURTH-GRADE TEACHER

There is no reason on earth why your children cannot be working on Wall Street the day after they finish college. This thought may never have occurred to you, or to them. I want to spell this out, so that all of you can share this dream.

Because it's not easy to survive in the financial industry, Wall Street firms are constantly looking for new talent. You've got to have the people skills of Oprah and the stamina of Michael Jordan and be as quick on your feet as Chris Rock is with his mouth. No one expects a recent college grad to know much about the stock market. Nonetheless, investment firms constantly scour campuses for young recruits. Why not your kids?

Here's a peek at what goes on in the households of the wealthy. A father asks his high school student, "What would you like to do for a living?" The teen's answer is taken very seriously. If the reply is "I'd like to work on Wall Street," the father places some calls to friends in brokerage houses and other Wall Street–related firms. "Any chance you can take my kid on for the summer?" Dad asks.

Wealthy people maintain a "favor bank" for each other. They hire each other's kids, pass along information about jobs, and generally give each other a leg up. They don't do this with any particular goal in mind; helping out your friends just comes naturally. Children from low-income families obviously do not have this advantage. But there is a way to make up for that lack.

Impress upon your kids the importance of getting into the best college they can possibly attend. These schools are visited each year by the top investment firms looking for new talent. Once your kids have made it onto the ivy-walled campus, teach them the three most important words they'll hear in their college careers (no, not "All Night Rave"): *"Career counseling office."*

This group of professionals is hired by the university for the sole purpose of getting jobs for the students who attend that school. They do this in several ways. One is to let students know when a key employer is coming to visit campus, then arranging interviews between the employers and the college students. These interviews are for both summer internships and full-time positions. Your kids can level the playing field with the wealthy kids early on by going to the career counseling office during their freshman year and explaining exactly what kind of career they want to have.

Believe it or not, minority job candidates and struggling lower-to-middle-income individuals are considered prizes for these employers. Now, you and I can question their motives until the sun comes up. They might be courting our kids out of some sense of corporate guilt, or because they want to have a rainbow coalition of faces to print on their employment brochures. Perhaps they want to have some African-American or Latino faces in the office to attract wealthy African-American or Latino clients. Don't concern yourself with their reasons.

Welcome to Wall Street!

The bottom line is that they want to hire our kids. The only way they can do so is to get to know them. The career counseling office is the connection between the first-rate, top-notch employers and your shining star. Becoming a familiar face in the career counseling office is as important as any lesson learned in the classroom, and a lot more important than anything your child will do in a social setting.

The other function of the career counseling office is to match up current students with well-connected alumni looking to help out current students. Wise college students seek out alumni who work in their desired field and ask to come in for an "informational interview." This interview is simply an opportunity to go to the firm, meet the alumnus (the person who graduated from their college), see the workplace, and *be seen*. When an employer sees someone like your son or daughter, strings are pulled, arrangements are made, and before you know it, job offers happen.

Your high school–age children should already be thinking about what they want to do with their lives. Does Johnny want to go into finance? Does Sarah want to be an engineer? Does Shaquille want to be a lawyer? Once your kids have a rough idea of what career they want, they can research which colleges provide the best training and education in that field.

Privileged children do it backward. First they choose their college, usually based on their family's alumni loyalties or on the school's prestige, as opposed to any particular program the school offers. For them, college is a four- or five-year party.

Some children from wealthy families don't make career decisions until they have been out of college for three or four years! Why? Because they can afford to. They move back home with their parents, or they travel, or they take a job teaching English overseas for a year. Yes, the children of the wealthy have it great, except for one thing: the clock is ticking and they are wasting time, not moving forward with the business of becoming adults.

Our kids need to be adults from the first day they hit the college campus. They have no time to waste. Impress upon your high school–age children that in college they will make the leap from the limited employment opportunities in their neighborhoods to whatever career they can imagine. When children from lower-income families go to college, they need to be told repeatedly by their parents that this is their opportunity to become whatever they want. The help will be available. The career counseling office will open its doors. Alumni are standing by, ready to give them a hand up. But it is the sole responsibility of your children to seek out these options and maximize their effectiveness. And it is your solemn obligation as a parent to inform your children of the possibilities that exist in college, and then to supervise their career searches. When you speak with your college-age children, ask when they last visited the career counseling office. Question them about interviews. Inquire about how they plan to spend their summer vacation. Nag them. Annoy them. This is the last chance you'll get, so milk it for all it's worth! Their futures are riding on it.

Children from low-income homes are often the first generation to attend college. Don't let them fall into the trap of wondering if they really belong there. They *do*. They have demonstrated their potential either in the classroom or on standardized achievement tests, or there is just something about them on a personal level that interviewing committee members of a school have recognized. Make sure they take advantage not just of the classes and the social life that college offers, but also the career possibilities.

Right now, a lot of popular sitcoms on TV purport to show life in college. They focus, generally, on wealthy kids and the social lives they enjoy in the dorms. While the wealthy kids are out there messing around and messing up, your kids need to be in the library, in the classroom, and, above all, in the career counseling office. Have I made myself clear?

CHAPTER 16

Your Kid's Future in the NBA?

It is important to educate children about money matters as soon as possible so that they can wisely plan the use of their money for their future. Since longevity of money invested in the American economy is more important than the amount of money invested, the earlier children can begin to wisely invest their money, the better. It is especially important in the inner city, where every adult does not have a bank account or knowledge of how to make their money work for them. If children learn at an early age how to use their money, they then become adults who know how to make their finances work for them.

AARON BARNER, THIRD-GRADE TEACHER

The child most "at risk" in the inner city is the child who appears to be doing well in school. That child is at risk of being taunted, embarrassed, and even beaten up by other kids who can't stand the idea that somebody might actually succeed in life.

If your children show signs of succeeding in school, you must do everything in your power to encourage them and help them deal with the negative peer pressure they will undoubtedly face. Help them find teachers who will mentor them as they seek to navigate the emotional maze that is high school. Or consider having your child educated in a magnet school, where peer pressure encourages academic success.

And consider this: a world of opportunity awaits your children at college—even before they're old enough to attend. Take your kids to visit the career counseling office at a nearby college or university. Although they are not specifically geared to assist high school students, any career counselor worth his or her salt would be impressed by a high school student paying a visit. (Who knows? Your kid may build a relationship with the counselor that helps him or her get into that school!) A career counselor will be more than happy to give your kids ideas on how to find after-schooljobs and internships, or simply to answer questions about a particular career. The counselor may even be able to offer advice on how to tailor an application for a particular school or career.

The more your kids are exposed to the opportunities that come with a college degree, the more likely they are to work hard to reach their goals. Most people—adults included—need to be shown what's possible in order to feel inspired or motivated. Our duty as parents is to show our kids as much as we can.

Encourage your children to write letters to leaders in your city to learn about their work. Their names will be listed at the local public library or on the Internet. Have your kids write to the head of the local electric company, lawyers in top law firms, and the CEOs of major businesses in the area. Don't worry about bothering these people or wasting their time. Top-level professionals always have the most help: assistants, secretaries, and public relations specialists.

Here's a sample of a letter your children could write. If possible, have them type the letter on nice paper. Check for spelling and punctuation errors.

Your Kid's Future in the NBA?

Dear Mr. or Ms. Jones:

I am a fifteen-year-old high school sophomore at Martin Luther King, Jr., High School. I intend to go to college in three years, and I am exploring career options at this time. Would it be possible for me to visit your office and learn a little bit about your business and what you do? I only need fifteen minutes of your time.

Thank you very much. I look forward to hearing from you.
Sincerely yours,
Jane Smith

Your kids might say, "Who's going to read a letter from me?" The answer is, everybody. While they may not hear from every single person they contact, your kids will find that the vast majority will be willing to meet with them or have another employee give them a tour of the business. Chances are, once your children have a positive experience on an informational interview, they'll want to write dozens more letters.

Have your child prepare for the visit by researching the company or at least the industry. Most companies, even small ones, have websites chock-full of information. The day of the visit, make sure your child dresses appropriately and goes armed with pen and notepad —and a resume, if she has one. (The visit may yield an internship or part-time job!) Have her write down any questions she may have going in; she should have many. (Remind her to inquire about possible scholarships the company offers.) Not only does this maximize the benefit of the visit, but it also makes her look prepared and organized to a potential employer. Remind your child to ask for a business card, then have her follow up with a thank-you note to every person she met. If business cards aren't available, she can write down the information on her trusty notepad. Along with her thank you, she can include follow-up questions that she's thought of since the visit. Your child may even develop a relationship with a new-found career mentor, in which case she'll have a great contact for a letter of reference for college applications.

Birds of a feather flock together, and that is certainly true for business leaders. Businesspeople are constantly meeting at lunches and all sorts of industry gatherings. If a worthy young person comes to the attention of one of them, word of mouth will soon bring her to the attention of them all. Get your children into the loop as early as possible. They'll be meeting people who can inspire and assist them as they make their way forward in life.

CHAPTER 17

The Learning Never Ends

Being financially literate will help me to manage my bank accounts, will teach me how to invest my money, and will prevent anyone from financially taking advantage of me. Learning about financial literacy in the Banking on Our Future Program is as important to me as learning to read and write.

FELICIA COOK, FIFTH-GRADE STUDENT

This book is only the beginning! In this chapter, we'll explore other ways you and your children can continue to grow in financial literacy. We'll look at methods to make your family financial summits interesting and exciting. And we'll also include a list of informative and noteworthy books that offer different perspectives on how to increase your financial knowledge.

CONTEND, DON'T PRETEND

One of the differences between the wealthy (the contenders) and people who just want to live wealthy (the pretenders) is how much time they spend studying investments. A lot of people who make decent money never get wealthy because they misallocate their time. Even in middle-class homes, people spend more time deciding what car to buy than planning for retirement. A car will last three years if you lease it, five or six years if you take decent care of it, and ten or twelve years if you take excellent care of it. But a savings and retirement program will take care of you for the rest of your life.

If you and your children want to enjoy financial self-sufficiency, follow the example of the contenders and begin to study money. The following list contains books that may interest you and your kids. Each covers different aspects of money and/or business.

1. *How to Have a 48-Hour Day* by Don Aslett

Aslett teaches efficiency tools that help people get much more done in the course of a day. It's not about working harder; it's about working smarter.

2. *How I Raised Myself from Failure to Success in Selling* by Frank Bettger

Business is all about selling. This book, written by a former major-league baseball player, may seem "old school" to your kids, but for my money there is no better guide to the art of selling!

3. *Barron's Profiles of American Colleges*

This huge paperback describes entrance standards, scholarship information, educational opportunities, and campus life for more than 1,600 colleges and universities across the nation. I suggest that you buy this book and leave it out where your kids are likely to pick it up and leaf through it. Let them start imagining themselves as college students!

4. *What Color Is Your Parachute?* by Richard Nelson Bolles

This is the bible for anyone looking for a job—but it's much more than that. It shows how to choose a career that maximizes your service to the world. Every college career counseling office in America has this book—why shouldn't your kids have it as well?

5. *How to Win Friends and Influence People* by Dale Carnegie

This classic, from the world-renowned business guru, teaches how to get along with others and maximize the effectiveness of relation-

The Learning Never Ends

ships. For decades, this book has been the mainstay of social relationships among successful people. Give your kids access to that information and those skills.

6. *The Wealthy Barber* by David Chilton
The story of a man who cuts hair in an ordinary neighborhood outside of Detroit. What's unusual about this barber is that he's a millionaire! While he works, he explains strategies for becoming wealthy, going into detail about everything from investing and savings to insurance and home ownership.

7. *The Richest Man in Babylon* by George Clason
A guide to saving, paying down debt, and investing, written in the 1920s but just as applicable today. Clason wrote the book as a series of parables from ancient times, and it's very enjoyable.

8. *MoneyLove* by Jerry Gilles
This book helps you understand how you think and feel about money. Surprisingly, our mindset about money is even more important than hard work as a determinant in our success.

9. *Think and Grow Rich, a Black Choice* by Dennis Kimbro and Napoleon Hill
Until his death in 1970, Hill was the number-one teacher and preacher of success in America. Kimbro outlines Hill's belief that blacks should not permit barriers such as racism, discrimination, and lack of opportunity to be self-defeating obstacles. The book covers both Hill's laws of success and Kimbro's vast knowledge of business. Countless black Americans have extolled the knowledge within these pages, including Spike Lee, Jesse Jackson, and Oprah Winfrey.

10. *Minding the Store* by Stanley Marcus
An eye-opening treasure trove of secrets on how to succeed. Marcus details his rise from ordinary businessman to founder of Neiman Marcus, perhaps the greatest luxury store in America. He explains the sales strategies that made his store so successful.

Banking on Our Future

11. *Peterson's Two-Year Colleges*

A guide to two-year college programs across the country. Many graduates of America's top four-year colleges and universities began their post–high school education at two-year colleges. Find out how here.

12. *The Dynamic Laws of Prosperity* by Katherine Ponder

Reverend Ponder, a Unity Church minister, teaches the spiritual underpinnings of success. Delightful and easy to read, this book offers a wealth of inspiring information.

13. *The Millionaire Next Door*
by Thomas J. Stanley and William D. Danko

Subtitled *The Surprising Secrets of America's Wealthy*, this fascinating peek into how the other half lives explains how wealthy people become wealthy . . . and stay that way.

14. *A Voice in the Unseen* by Ron Suskind

The beautifully written and extremely moving story of a young man from inner-city Washington, D.C., who fights the odds and attends a summer program at M.I.T. and then Brown University.

15. *Resumes for Dummies* by Joyce Lain Kennedy

Everything your kids (and you!) need to know about creating resumes that get jobs. You'll also learn why resumes often have little or nothing to do with getting many kinds of jobs—and how to get those jobs as well!

You can find all of these books in your public library or local bookstore. Consider having your kids each read a chapter of a different book and then report what they learned at family financial summits. Use the information as a springboard for discussion.

Although the information in these books is freely available, the only people who seem to take advantage of it are people who are already wealthy or are on their way up! It's time to get your kids on the path to a better life, and the only way to scale the heights in our society is with information.

The Learning Never Ends

Louis Mandel, dean of the University of Buffalo School of Management, laments that many young people are ill-prepared to deal with money management.

> Millions of American teenagers graduate from high school every year without a basic understanding of how to manage their money. As they venture out from under their parents' protection for the first time, what awaits these young adults is an increasingly complex society that asks that they make immediate and sometimes irreversible financial decisions—decisions that will likely impact their livelihoods for years to come. . . . The consequences can be quite severe. Debilitating debt, clumsy money management, poor retirement planning, and even bankruptcy—this is what the financial future holds for many American teenagers because they were never given proper, if any, instruction in the basics of personal finance. ("Why Johnny Can't Balance a Checkbook," *UB Today*, Winter 1999)

Please note that Mandel did not say inner-city teenagers or lower-income teenagers or teenagers who are black or Latino. Mandel is talking about *American* teenagers. In other words, very few parents properly educate their children about money. Mandel goes on to discuss how, in 1997, he administered a personal finance exam to 1,500 high school seniors nationwide. These students were asked basic personal finance questions regarding the very topics we've been discussing in this book: money management, saving and investing, and spending and credit. Overall, only 10 percent of the students who took the exam received a grade of "C" or better. Mandel writes, "These results indicate that America's teenagers are heading down a path toward financial difficulty at the very least." He's got that one right. If kids can't handle money, they won't be able to handle life. Now, thanks to the information that you are able to share with them, your kids will know what awaits them in their financial future.

CHAPTER 18

A Vision for America . . . and for You

It is key for kids to have an awareness about money, what it buys, how to save it. What I have not done is link money and spending to behavior. What I need to do is create habits for my kids.

ANGELICA JOHNSON, MOTHER OF THREE,

AT A BANKING ON OUR FUTURE EVENT

At Operation HOPE I talk a lot about building a new generation of what I call the stakeholder class: a new class of Americans, lodged between the working class and the middle class; a stepping-stone to the new middle class. The stakeholder class is less about making more money, and much more about *making better decisions with the money you make.*

My purpose in this book has been to show how you and your children can become stakeholders in American society—people who *invest themselves* in their own future; who *make investments* in real estate, stocks, bonds, mutual funds, and the other tools for acquiring wealth; and who *are invested in* economic life instead of standing on the sidelines.

After observing my brothers and sisters growing up in low-to moderate-income African-American communities, I am convinced that all Americans have the brains, the intellect, the passion, and the commitment to succeed in life. We are not lagging because of a lack of what it takes, but because we are *not doing* what it takes! Even the Bible speaks to this precious bit of economic advice! The Greek word for poor, as used by Jesus, is *poucos*, which means non-productivity. Being poor doesn't mean you don't have anything; it means you aren't *doing* anything.

I have been there.

I remember when I was in my late teens and early twenties and had made one too many financial missteps, due to my ego and lack of good business sense.

I wanted to profile, be the man and look the man! I learned the hard way that there is a BIG difference between looking successful and being successful. A BIG difference between business and busy-ness. A big difference between working hard and working smart.

I remember all of my bad decisions, and I pretty much knew when I was making one:

Buying $1,000 worth of stereo equipment when I didn't have a $1,000 mutual fund to my name.

Leasing the Mercedes-Benz (profiling) instead of buying a Honda (being practical). I didn't have the down payment for a Mercedes, and I could scrape up the payment if I carried only liability insurance and used my credit card to buy dinner two nights a week. The bottom line is that I had no business on a Mercedes-Benz car lot, aside from perhaps going to work there to sell them to people who *could* afford to buy them!

Or spending money because it "made me feel good" (a sure sign that we all need a little psychotherapy as one of our Christmas gifts). What I really needed to do was dump the girlfriend who was causing me nothing but stress, along with the dinner tabs I could not afford, and invest some of that money instead in my savings account, a mutual fund, my retirement 401(k), and, if there was any left over, some serious therapy!

Been there. Done that.

No. I wasn't crazy. But the definition of insanity is "doing the same thing over and over again, but expecting a different outcome."

We, each of us, need to end that spending cycle and join the stakeholder-class movement. Instead of focusing on making more money, we need to focus more of our time and energy on learning the lessons of life, and making better decisions with the money we make. And then we must pass this attitude down to our children, along with the other invaluable principles and values of life we teach them.

We are the only country in the world that is home to every ethnic group. Our two most ethnically diverse states are California and New York. Now guess which two states are also the most economically prosperous. That's right: California and New York. That's the power of diversity!

I've spent the last ten years telling businesspeople and politicians that they cannot do business with people they don't respect or understand. I've tried to serve as a middle ground between the contented rich and the working poor in our society, helping them sing a chorus of "Getting to Know You." Thanks to Operation HOPE, the banking world, the business world, and the political leadership of this country are a lot more aware of the economic power and the economic potential of the inner city. I wouldn't go so far as to say that they're standing there with open arms, ready to embrace you, your dreams, and your children's dreams. But at least they're ready to do business with us.

Now it's your turn. We're not just talking about rights. We're talking about responsibilities.

It's your responsibility to seize the power that awaits you! This book offers the tools you and your children need to become economically empowered. Operation HOPE is all about empowering people: moving people from check-cashing customers to banking customers, from renters to homeowners, from small-business dreamers to small-business owners, from minimum-wage workers to living-wage workers with new-economy job skills. Knowledge is power—and now that you've got the knowledge, it's time to take responsibility for your economic life in a brand-new way. Teach these lessons to your children. Give them a mindset of success, not dependency. Of making it on their own.

Former HUD Secretary and Operation HOPE board member Jack Kemp and I are partnering a program we call the Inner-City Partnership for New-Economy Jobs. We have brought the University of California, Los Angeles, into the inner city of Los Angeles. Our Cyber Café, which was opened in 2000 by then–Vice President Al Gore, is a computer bank that links South Central to UCLA and Smartforce, the leading distance learning company in the nation. As of this writing, we have partnered with E-Trade Bank and are expanding the Cyber Café program to Washington, D.C.; soon we'll expand it to other cities as well.

The Cyber Café is more than just a place to enjoy a cup of coffee. It's an economic literacy program that educates young people so they can get a leg up and find a place in the new economy.

We have three banking centers in South Central L.A., where there are no other banks. Our banking centers are not nonprofit handouts. They are for-profit subsidiaries of our nonprofit operation. Wells Fargo has invested $2 million. Washington Mutual has invested close to $2 million. Hawthorne Savings has invested $2 million. Union Bank of California is a partner in all three locations. We used part of the money to build inner-city Cyber Cafés, and part of it to connect to UCLA Extension, which issues degrees in basic information technology.

When you finish the eight-point program, which includes the UCLA training, you get a certificate from UCLA Extension. Then you go through corporate orientation training and a corporate internship for forty hours; you complete credit counseling, case management, and technical assistance. If you finish all that training and fulfill your commitment, we'll guarantee you a job at a living wage, moving you from $6 an hour to $16 an hour.

Does it surprise you that every class, with no advertising at all, is oversubscribed? And this is just one program! I urge you to search your community, wherever you live, to discover the resources that await you and your children. And by all means contact us so that we can determine how Operation HOPE can directly serve you and your neighbors. Since 1992, we have had well over 223,000 borrowers, customers, and clients of Operation HOPE in South Central L.A. But if you don't live near an Operation HOPE center, consider this book your personal guide to economic success. As I love to say, we believe in James Brown's version of affirmative action, "Open the door, and I'll get it myself!"

There's a new mandate for this country, a new responsibility for its leaders. The shame of the twentieth century was racism. The shame of the twenty-first century will be poverty. The rich are getting richer, the poor are getting poorer, and it's hard to be middle class. Wherever you have anarchy, you have a country divided between the very rich and the very poor. You have a country where there's no way for the very poor to become very rich, so *since they know they can't make it, they feel they might as well just take it.* A society is at its greatest risk from those individuals who have no stake in it.

But you and I cannot sit around waiting for political, business, and banking leaders to wave a magic wand and suddenly make everything beautiful. Life doesn't work that way! We can't expect government or business or anyone else to solve our problems. That's why I've sought to provide you with the information in this book. Let's put it this way: the business community is now more *receptive* to doing business with you and more open to including you and your children in the American dream. But it's up to you to take advantage of that receptivity and openness by taking action on your own behalf—and teaching your children how to do the same thing!

The War on Poverty failed. America, to its credit, spent billions of dollars trying to eradicate poverty. Didn't work. In retrospect, we see that it *couldn't* have worked. You can't make poverty go away by writing a check. Poverty can be eliminated only by transforming the poor into stakeholders in their community. Yes, the doors had to be pried open . . . first by leaders like Martin Luther King Jr. and organizations like the NAACP and the National Urban League, by the

A Vision for America . . . and for You

War on Poverty, and now by organizations like Operation HOPE. But now that the doors are open, it's up to you and yours to march on through!

America has retreated from its commitment to help the poor, and the proof of that is the gated community. In case you've never seen a gated community, let me tell you about it: a community of very nice homes, pools, tennis courts, athletic facilities, maybe even a golf course or two. And it's surrounded by a fence (with a gate). To keep *you* out.

Sure, you can enter a gated community . . . by hiding in the trunk of a homeowner's car. Or by working as a cleaning person in the home of a wealthy resident. Or by going to clean out the pool or mow the golf course. But otherwise, the gate is closed to keep you — and your children — out.

What's the real message of a gated community? It's people saying, "Can't solve it, can't deal with it, I'm giving up, I'm taking care of myself." People today aren't interested in solving societal problems; they just want to get home to their DVD players. Am I being unfair? Well then, *you* give *me* a better explanation for all those gates!

My friend, love and hate are not the problem. Rich people don't hate the poor, and our problems wouldn't be solved if somehow we could get them to love us. The real problem today is indifference.

On the whole, people don't care whether you succeed or fail, get rich or go broke, live or die. And they sure don't care about your children, either! If they did, they'd help give your kids the same quality schools they give their own children.

Yes, indifference is the problem. Since the wealthy are indifferent to the plight of the poor and working class, it's more important than ever that you gain the knowledge, skills, and tools you need to take good financial care of your family.

America is moving from race-based and place-based discrimination to class-based discrimination, rooted in education and access to information. In other words, people today are less likely to care about the color of your skin or where you live. They just want to know, "Are you educated? Can you handle the job? Do you have the training? Do you know what it means to hold down a job?" The danger we face is not racial or facial discrimination, but discrimination based on lack of education.

My coauthor, Michael Levin, tells the story of driving cross-country a few years back and going to a dance club in Abilene, Texas. A white girl in her late teens was out on the dance floor, showing a young black man, about her age, how to do a particular dance step. No one at the club, black or white, seemed to be paying attention. Michael realized the fact that the two dancers could go unnoticed represented a huge shift in thinking. Earlier in his life—and perhaps in yours as well—that young black man might have been punished or even killed for daring to step on a dance floor with a white girl.

Among the young, race is much less an issue than it was for their parents, or their grandparents. But that doesn't mean all our problems are solved. It just means that the battleground has shifted . . . from civil rights to *silver rights*, as I like to say. Civil rights were won by blacks and whites working together—in communities, in churches, on Freedom Rides, in voter registration drives, on the national news. *Silver rights* are won at the kitchen table, one family at a time!

In the new century, the tool to eradicate poverty will be education. Wealth will be decided by access to information and education. A more educated populace makes better decisions. People will act to create wealth for themselves . . . and *conserve*, or protect it, for themselves and their families.

Conservative financial decision making means buying the Honda instead of profiling with the Mercedes. This means *becoming* wealthy instead of simply trying to look the part. This means (dare I say it?) *delaying gratification* instead of getting and spending and getting and spending. It means putting money into the *invisible necessities of life*—car insurance, life insurance, savings vehicles —instead of into the *visible luxuries of life*, like fancy cars, fancy clothes, and fancy toys.

A Vision for America . . . and for You

Elsewhere in this book I provide a list of other books that you and your family can use to continue developing your economic awareness. One of my favorite books on the list is Thomas J. Stanley and William D. Danko's *The Millionaire Next Door*, which shows how wealthy America *gets that way*. Most of the millionaires in this country don't drive super-expensive, showy cars and don't wear expensive clothing. Instead, they got rich—and stay rich—because they *lived within their means* while they were on the way up . . . and live below their means now that they're rich.

Stanley and Danko pose a question: why won't a millionaire let you ride in his Rolls-Royce? The surprising answer: because most rich people don't drive Rolls-Royces! Instead of showing everyone how rich they are, they live modestly, for the most part. Instead of working to make money to show off, they let their money work for them. That's what I want for you and your kids. I want your children to learn how to *create and conserve* wealth, instead of falling prey to the ghetto mentality that says, "It's more important to *look* rich than to *be* rich."

When the L.A. riots took place in 1992, most people hit the streets and started tearing up something because they were frustrated. I was angry, but I took that anger and used it constructively. I made it a passion and focused it on eradicating poverty and changing the world through Operation HOPE. Operation HOPE is not male or female, Republican or Democrat. It is a holistic approach to eradicating poverty and solving problems in our society, and I want you to be a part of it.

I believe that in this country we stand on the cusp of a movement for change. For the first time, America will be a country composed of a majority of minorities. People don't care whether leaders are white, black, red, brown, or yellow, as long as they can produce some *green*. That takes education. Educate your children to be financially responsible—and to be leaders.

I wish you love, I wish you riches, I wish you spiritual success. On behalf of everyone at Operation HOPE, I wish you and yours hope for a beautiful, happy, financially rewarding life!

CHAPTER 19

Bring "Banking on Our Future" to Your School

Financial literacy is such a powerful tool for all people to learn about, especially children. It teaches children how to make wise decisions while they are young to improve their financial life as they grow older. Participating in the Banking on Our Future Program has given me a chance to increase my personal knowledge of saving money and how money can work for me through investments. This is something that will help me for the rest of my life.

CLIFFORD THORNTON, FIFTH-GRADE STUDENT

If you found the ideas in this book useful, we'd love to share them with your classmates and teachers by visiting your school through the Banking on Our Future Program. Or if you need help with taxes, check-cashing questions, cleaning up credit ratings, home loans, or college scholarships, please contact us:

Operation HOPE, Inc.
Banking on Our Future
707 Wilshire Boulevard, 30th Floor
Los Angeles, California 90017
(213) 891-2900   (877) 592-HOPE (toll free)
www.operationhope.org

APR (ANNUAL PERCENTAGE RATE) The service charge you pay for a loan or credit card.

ASSET Something you own, such as a house, a car, or money in a bank account.

BOUNCED CHECK A check that doesn't go through because you don't have enough money in the account or overdraft protection.

CALL An *option* you buy if you think a stock will go higher. Although you can make a good deal of money with a call in a short amount of time, buying one is not advised if you are new to trading.

CLEARED CHECK A check for which you have enough money in your account. The money is deducted from your account and added to the account of the payee.

DEBIT CARD A bank card that functions both as an ATM card, allowing you to withdraw money from ATM machines, and as a credit card, allowing you to make purchases with it in stores or restaurants. Unlike with a credit card, however, when you use a debit card to make a purchase, the money is deducted immediately from your bank balance.

DOWN PAYMENT The initial amount of money used to secure a large purchase, such as a home or car.

EQUITY The amount of the value of an item such as a house, car, or boat that you own, minus the amount that you still owe the bank.

FICA Another common form of deduction from your pay.

FICO The ratings system used for credit histories.

GPA (GRADE POINT AVERAGE) The average score of a student's grades, usually measured in high school on a letter-based scale (A, B, C, D, or F) and in higher education on a 4.0 scale (with 4.0 being the highest).

Glossary

GRANT Money for education that you don't have to pay back, unlike a student loan.

INTEREST The money you pay the bank or other lender for the privilege of borrowing their money.

INTEREST RATE The percentage of the amount of the loan that you must pay back each year. For example, if you borrow $100 at 6 percent annual interest, you must pay back $6 for every year you keep the money.

IRA (INDIVIDUAL RETIREMENT ACCOUNT) A tax-free form of saving that can be used not only for retirement but also for education and other purposes.

MUTUAL FUND A form of saving that yields higher returns than a savings account, although the risks are greater.

NASDAQ An electronic "place" for trading stocks. Generally speaking, the companies whose stocks are traded on the NASDAQ are newer, smaller, and more high-tech oriented. If your kids are into anything to do with technology or the web, chances are the companies they are most interested in are listed on the NASDAQ.

NEW YORK STOCK EXCHANGE (NYSE) The primary location of stock trading. Every business day, individuals and institutions buy and sell shares of corporations at the New York Stock Exchange. (You can learn more about the way the stock exchange works—its intricate system for matching up buyers and sellers—by visiting its website, *www.nyse.com*.)

OPTION A risky investment method in which an individual bets on the direction (up or down) a stock will go. (See also *call* and *put*.)

OVERDRAFT PROTECTION A bank's agreement to cover checks you write against a checking account even if you don't have enough money in the account. You still have to pay that money back, plus interest!

PORTFOLIO The collection of stocks an individual owns. If you have shares of stock in ten or twenty different companies, that is your portfolio of stocks.

PROBATE The process by which a court declares a will valid.

Glossary

PUT An *option* you buy if you think a stock will go lower. Although you can make a good deal of money with a put in a short amount of time, buying one is not advised if you are new to trading.

REDLINING The now-illegal bank practice of never loaning money for homes in certain low-income areas.

SCHOLARSHIP Money for education you don't have to pay back, like a grant.

SHARE A piece of ownership in a corporation.

WORK-STUDY An arrangement whereby a student receives money for education in exchange for holding down a student job.

Operation HOPE (*www.operationhope.org*): The organization founded in the wake of the 1992 Los Angeles civil unrest to bring banking to the inner city and foster economic literacy and self-sufficiency among inner-city children

Banking on Our Future (*www.bankingonourfuture.org*): Inter-active website for learning the fundamentals of finance

CREDIT HISTORY

Equifax (*www.equifax.com*): Credit reporting company

FINANCIAL

Morningstar (*www.morningstar.com*): Database of mutual funds

American Century (*www.americancentury.com*): Database of mu-tual funds

New York Stock Exchange (*www.nyse.com*): The primary stock trading location

EDUCATIONAL

FinAid (*www.finaid.org*): Financial aid information

College Is Possible (*www.collegeispossible.com*): Financial aid in-formation

Fastweb (*www.fastweb.com*): Scholarship database

HOME OWNERSHIP

Realtor.com (*www.realtor.com*): Information about how to pur-chase a home, mortgage calculators, the cost of homes across the country, and much more

ACKNOWLEDGMENTS

We wish to thank our outstanding team at Beacon Press, as exemplified by our editor, Tisha Hooks, whose idea—and dream—this book was, and editor Joanne Wyckoff. We hope that our effort has lived up to their expectations.

Special thanks to our literary agent, Colleen Mohyde, without whose indefatigable efforts and great wisdom this book would never have come to be.

We also thank the entire Operation HOPE staff and the volunteers, teachers, and students of Banking on Our Future who shared their experiences with us. In order to protect the privacy of some of the young people, we have changed their names or combined the experiences of several students into one story.

We also acknowledge Jenna Robbins and Melody La Vasani for their diligent work in preparing the manuscript for publication.

Index

Index

Index

Index

on credit cards, 94, 95
information about, online, 95
on loans, 96, 98, 101, 113
paid by banks, 48
paid by credit unions, 48
on secured vs. unsecured debt, 98
for teenagers, 94, 96
Internal Revenue Service (IRS), 32
Internet. *See* information, online
internships, finding, 138
interviews
help with, 134
see also informational interviews
investment(s)
home ownership as, 99–100, 108
learning about, 127–29, 141–42, 143
of savings, 70, 130
savings as, 48, 49, 146
the stock market and, 127–31, 146
see also Individual Retirement Account
IRA. *See* Individual Retirement Account

jobs
after college, 134–36
books about, 142, 144
drawbacks of, for teenagers, 15–16
in the financial industry, 133
finding after-school, 138
information technology, help for, 149

Kennedy, Joyce Lain, *Resumes for Dummies*, 144
kids
accounts in names of, 73
encouraging ambition in, 44–45, 135–36
financial goals for, 44–45
financial record keeping by, 41, 79–80
financial values of, 58–61
guardianship of, 118, 119
mentors for, 138, 139

parents' health care provisions and, 117, 121
parents' wills and, 117
talking to, about money, 39, 45
teaching money management to, 7, 145
see also teenagers
Kimbro, Dennis, and Napoleon Hill, *Think and Grow Rich, a Black Choice*, 143

Lasser, J. K., as publisher of tax information, 83
letters
on money matters. *See* correspondence
thank-you, importance of, 139
writing, as networking, 138–40
lien, for nonpayment of taxes, 89
Lifetime Learning Credit, 114
loan
bank, 49, 50, 95
car, 95, 96, 98
for college expenses, 113, 114
criteria for, 109
establishing a good credit record with, 95
home, 98, 106, 109, 154
home equity, 100–101, 131–32
interest rates on, 101, 113
principal of, 101
as profitable for lenders, 98
secured, mortgage as, 102
for tax payment, 89
see also debt; interest rates

Marcus, Stanley, *Minding the Store*, 143
medical expenses, filing system for, 32
meetings, family, and finances, 42–44, 46
mentors, for your kids, 138, 139
merit, and financial aid for college, 113
minorities, as sought-after job candidates, 134
money
attitudes toward, 13–15, 17, 22, 143

Index

managing. *See* financial literacy; money management
money management
 family financial summit meetings and, 42–45, 46
 goals of, 152
 importance of, 145, 146, 148
 record keeping and, 23–24, 32–33, 41, 80
money order, as an alternative to checks, 71
Morningstar (website), 130, 158
mortgage payments, 101, 158
mutual funds, 130–31, 146, 158

networking, 134, 135, 138–40
New York Stock Exchange, website, 158

open house, described, 102–3
Operation HOPE
 address of, 154
 checkbook balancing and, 34
 check cashing and, 71–72, 154
 for college scholarships, 154
 credit counseling from, 27, 154
 for credit record errors, 96, 154
 goals of, 10, 150, 153
 for home loans, 154
 and money management decision making, 66
 in purchasing a home, 101, 105, 110–11, 131
 redlining and, 109, 111
 taxation and, 89, 154
 see also Banking on Our Future program
overdraft
 fees, 91
 protection, 74

payments, minimum
 on bills, 31
 on credit cards, 25

payroll deductions. *See* deductions, for taxes
peer pressure
 and academic success, 137–38
 and buying consumer goods, 5, 60–61
 and financial values, 16–17, 20
Pell Grant, 114
Perkins Loan Program, 114
Peterson's Two-Year Colleges, 144
piggy banks, 46
points programs, as introduction to credit cards, 57–58
Ponder, Katherine, *The Dynamic Laws of Prosperity*, 144
Prentice-Hall, as publisher of tax information, 83
privacy concerns
 affinity programs and, 58
 online information and, 58, 59
probate
 defined, 119
 importance of avoiding, 119–20
property, and secured debt, 97
proxy, health care, 120–23

Quicken personal finance computer program, 27, 34

real estate
 investing in, 131–32, 146, 158
 ownership of, 48
realtor
 website, 158
 see also broker, real estate
record keeping
 categories for, 23
 computer programs for, 27, 34
 importance of, for cash transactions, 71
 by kids, 41, 79–80
 method for, 31–33
 sharing, with the family, 40–42, 80
 spending patterns and, 23–24
 vs. budgeting, 26–27

Index

Index